The Oneness

EUNICE FORSON

The oneness

*Mystery behind the construction
of the Lampstand*

The **oneness**

Mystery behind the construction of the Lampstand

Cover and nterior Design by:
Chris Treccani
www.3dogcreative.net

The Mustard Seed
MINISTRIES

INTERCESSION *(noun)*

in-ter-sesh'-un (paga`) "to make intercession"; originally "to strike upon," or "against"; then in a good sense, "to assail anyone with petitions," "to urge," and when on behalf of another, "to intercede"

- The action of intervening on behalf of another.
- The act of using your influence to make someone in authority forgives someone else or save the person from punishment.
- The action of saying a prayer on behalf of another.

Genesis 1:1-3
The Story of Creation

In the beginning, when God created the universe, the earth was formless and desolate. The raging ocean that covered everything was engulfed in total darkness, and the Spirit of God was moving over the water. Then God commanded, "Let there be light"—and light appeared...

The Lampstand
Exodus 25: 31-40

"Make a lampstand of pure gold. Make its base and its shaft of hammered gold; its decorative flowers, including buds and petals, are to form one piece with it. Six branches shall extend from its sides, three from each side. Each of the six branches is to have three decorative flowers shaped like almond blossoms with buds and petals. The shaft of the lampstand is to have four decorative flowers shaped like almond blossoms with buds and petals. There is to be one bud below each of the three pairs of branches. The buds, the branches, and the lampstand are to be a single piece of pure hammered gold. Make seven lamps for the lampstand and set them up so that they shine toward the front. Make its tongs and trays of pure gold. Use seventy-five pounds of pure gold to make the lampstand and all this equipment. Take care to make them according to the plan that I showed you on the mountain.

Table of Contents

Preface   *xi*

Introduction   *xvii*

Part One   **The Word of the Lord**   **1**

Chapter One   To the Church   3

Chapter Two   A Vision of Christ   15

Chapter Three   Seven Golden Lampstands   29

Part Two   **The Hammering**   **43**

Chapter Four   Grafting   45

Chapter Five   Deposits of His Faith   79

Part Three   **The Messengers**   **89**

Chapter Six   The Watchful Servants   91

Part Four   **The Recipients**   109

Chapter Seven   The Banquet   111

Chapter Eight   The Invitation Message   139

Chapter Nine   Neither Hot nor Cold   161

Chapter Ten   The Blind Man   175

Part Five   **The Principles**   197

Chapter Eleven Of the Church   199

Chapter Twelve In the Church   209

Thanks for reading!   222

Other Books by Eunice Forson   224

PREFACE

This book series was birthed out of obedience. On July 28, 2010, I received a word of knowledge to write a book on *Discipline in the Church: The Plan of Perfect Intercession.* *Discipline in the Church* series offers an illustration of what needs to be done in the Church to bring unity when everything the Church incarnates brings division. The message of this book series is momentarily based on the Menorah—God's oneness of the Church. God has planned on bringing the whole Church together in His name (Genesis 1:1), and presently, the Church is divided.

This book warns the reader about the coming days, how to prepare our hearts in expectation, be watchful, and build a deeper relationship with God. It sends a warning to the Church about the Second Coming of Christ and what the Church will endure in the Name of Christ. This message, which is meant to unite the churches into one, must be simplified to the level that all would be able to read and understand. Therefore, for this reason, most of the Bible references are from the Good News Translation version. This message gives the reader a meaning of who Christ is. As a pharmacist with no background in theology, I wondered, *how will I do this?* But the Lord gave me His word and the wisdom to understand it. I am about to share God's spoken word with you as I received it.

Out-of-Body Experience

One night at the end of October, I had what I will classify as a dream. In the dream, I found myself translated in the spirit. I saw myself out of my body and roaming about in the street of a city. In my dream, as I walked along a road, I saw a great monster, horribly looking and massive, sitting on the left-hand side of the road. On my right, I saw deranged people, and individuals being shot at as well as murders being committed. The city descent into lawlessness; people with guns walked around threatening and bullying people into committing acts against their will. The city was out of place. Evil spirits were possessing innocent people's bodies.

These bodies were empty, and the spirits occupied the vacant space. In this strange world, everything was out of place, and violence was everywhere. I could see through the empty bodies. I seemed to possess a certain power that allowed me to overcome the spirit of the enemy. I had control because I was never approached as I roamed about the street of this city. The bodies stopped whatever they were doing the moment we made eye contact. The power I had, allowed me to seize their actions.

In one scene where I was walking down a path with other people, all heading in the same direction, one of the men was attacked by an evil spirit. The evil spirit wanted to take possession of his body, i.e., occupy the empty space in him. I stopped the spirit from taking residence in his body by raising my hand and commanding it to leave the man. "You cannot live in him," I stated firmly.

But then, I felt furious about the empty space in that man. In fact, I was angry at them all, asking them to protect themselves and prevent that from happening. It gave me a meaning that being filled with the Spirit of God makes it impossible for any evil spirit to take residence in your body. The Holy Spirit's fills leave you full. I wondered why these people have been left empty and not filled with the Spirit of God. The people literally had nothing inside of them. I could see through this man as he had been left without anything in him. He needed the Spirit of God in him, and at that instance, I covered him with my hand. I wandered around in the spirit for a long time. I didn't like the scenes that I saw, but at the same time, I was worried because Christ is coming, and the people were walking around empty without the Word of God in them.

I then asked God the following questions:

1. What is the meaning of this dream?

2. Why are the people empty? In that state, any spirit could take residence in them.
3. Why did you give me this dream?
4. Why is the ending of this world like this? Is it the ending of this world or the beginning of God's Kingdom when He will separate the light from the darkness? Genesis 1:1 says before the creation of the unison (oneness), the earth was formless and desolate. God's kingdom is about oneness—the universe.

God responded to my questions with the following answers:

- These are people with the word of God in their possession, but they are not filled with the word.
- They are the Church with His word in their hands, but His word is not in their hearts.
- They are shallow ({adj} *meaning: lacking intellectual or mental depth or subtlety; superficial*) in His word. His word needs to be implanted in them to fill their empty spaces up.
- The mission of the Church is to implant the word of God in the hearts of people.
- They are all empty vases, with nothing in them.
- The world is beating them to it.

The words of the Preacher, the son of David, king in Jerusalem. Vanity of vanities, says the Preacher, vanity of vanities! All is vanity. What does man gain by all the toil at which he toils under the sun? A generation goes, and a generation comes, but the earth remains forever (Ecclesiastes 1:1-4 ESV).

This book series titled *Discipline in the Church: The Plan of Perfect Intercession* contains an introduction and twelve chapters, and each chapter is an entire book on its own. Thirteen books make up this series on discipline in the Church. I trust that you will find this book very educational and spiritually inspiring.

Introduction

We live in a land of fear—fear about anything that comes across us when we are in denial of our faith. As a Christian community, we do not seem to practice the word of socialization. We tend to socialize with ourselves and our culture. Our tendency of not extending our culture to any other culture is our problem. We live within ourselves and do not include others. We reach out to people within the Christian community but not outside of it. We only look out for ours—not theirs. We are to be all for one—the Lord.

- Has it occurred to you that the Lord is for ALL?

He came for *all*—not just a single person. He came for the living soul, and as such, we have to commune together to bring His passion to pass.

- How will you know that without sharing ideas, one would pick a word or two of the Scripture from you?

Without shared interest, the world would be as it is till the Lord comes, and His coming depends on your oneness in Him. If you delay your communion with others, so will His coming be delayed. His association with you is easy, but His communion among you is delayed due to your unwillingness to commune with others, i.e., you are **pretentious**.

Communing with others expels the word "**depression**" from your life because through that communion, you educate God's people in the world about **His Word** and **His salvation**.

"Listen!" says Jesus. "I am coming soon! I will bring my rewards with me, to give to each one according to what he has done. I am the first and the last, the beginning and the end." Happy are those who wash their robes clean and so have the right to eat the fruit from the tree of life and to go through the gates into the city. But outside the city are the perverts and those who practice magic, the immoral and the murderers, those who worship idols and those who are liars both in word and deed.

"I, Jesus, have sent my angel to announce these things to you in the churches. I am descended from the family of David; I am the bright morning star." The Spirit and the Bride say, "Come!" Everyone who hears this must also say, "Come!" Come, whoever is thirsty; accept the water of life as a gift, whoever wants it (Revelation 22:12-17).

You tell them who God is and sing His songs to them that #He is the Almighty God, #the Great I Am, #Hallelujah!

Besides Him, there is no other; He is the "I Am that I Am." No one comes before or after Him. "I Am" is the Omnipotent, Omnipresent, and Omniscient God. He is the El-Shaddai; the God of Abraham; the King of kings; and the One Who knows all. He is the God of your ancestors, and they have proven to be wrong about His judgment. He is the Lord who brought them out of their distress when they had no one. He lifted them up in the times of their need. He does not judge according to your faith but judges you according to your heart. He is a principled God and "Just" is His name. He justifies you according to His will and makes you comfortable with His Word. He changes your situation for you although you do not yet know Him, but soon, you will learn His Word and will get to know Him.

Christ is like a single body, which has many parts; it is still one body, even though it is made up of different parts. In the same way, all of us, whether Jews or Gentiles, whether slaves or free, have been baptized into the one body by the same Spirit, and we have all been given the one Spirit to drink. For the body itself, is not made up of only one part, but of many parts. If the foot were to say, because I am not a hand, I don't belong to the body that would not keep it from being a part of the body. And if the ear were to say, because I am not an eye, I don't belong to the body that would not keep it from being a part of the body. If the whole body were just an eye, how could it hear? And if it were only an ear, how could it smell? As it is, however, God put every different part in the body just as he wanted it to be. There would not be a body if it were all only one part! As it is, there are many parts but one body.

So then, the eye cannot say to the hand, I don't need you! Nor can the head say to the feet, Well, I don't need you! ***On the contrary, we cannot do without the parts of the body that seem to be weaker; and those parts that we think aren't worth very much are the ones which we treat with greater care; while the parts of the body which don't look very nice are treated with special modesty,*** *which the more beautiful parts do not need. God himself has put the body together in such a way as to give greater honour to those parts that need it. And so there is no division in the body, but all its different parts have the same concern for one another. If one part of the body suffers, all the other parts suffer with it; if one part is praised, all the other parts share its happiness.*

1 Corinthians 12:12-26

God put things together, and no one else does. He has dedicated His Church to the world, and no one has. He is the One to come, and as He approaches His days of His coming,

He is going to set His Church in order and everyone must give honor to Him. He is the great I Am, and He intends to coach His people before He comes in order to set His Church right.

God will stir up a lot of confusion in the Body of Christ, and through that confusion, He will birth His Faithful Church. He intends to move His Church onto the earth, but He cannot until all His people are free of their misery. As He teaches His word, people will understand it and change their minds as they progress through it, i.e., **propaganda**.

A day is coming when people will sing, I praise you, Lord! You were angry with me, but now you comfort me and are angry no longer. God is my saviour; I will trust Him and not be afraid. The Lord gives me power and strength; He is my saviour. As fresh water brings joy to the thirsty, so God's people rejoice when He saves them (Isaiah 12:1-3).

Sing the Lord's songs to them in desperate need, in other words, sing the Lord's praises to them. Elevate God in their presence and they will know who He is. **The Just shall be satisfied!**

He shall see the labour of His soul, and be satisfied. By His Knowledge My Righteous Servant shall justify many, for He shall bear their iniquities (Isaiah 53:11).

---

*Tweet this: This is a word to the Christian:
"Live according to His Word and let His
salvation come to others in need of them."*

Live according to His will in Jesus Christ, and that way, people's lives will change and manifest His name. As Jesus said in the Scriptures, He has come to heal the land. The land was cursed by God in Genesis 3:17-19 because of man's disobedience. Man was the land (earth) that was cursed because it was from that ground that he was formed. When God pronounced the curse on the ground, that curse was directly directed to man; therefore, all of his generations are cursed. All those who will come out of the ground (earth) will be a curse according to His will.

*And He said to the man, you listened to your wife and ate the fruit which I told you not to eat. Because of what you have done, **the ground will be under a curse.** You will have to work hard all your life to make it produce enough food for you. **It will produce weeds and thorns,** and you will have to eat wild plants. You will have to work hard and sweat to make the soil produce anything, until you go back to the soil from which you were formed. You were made from soil, and you will become soil again.* (Genesis 3:17-19).

God first provided an escape route before pronouncing the curse on man. He provided man with grace through the offspring of the woman by removing the fig leaves that Adam and Eve had covered themselves with. He clothed our nakedness with the righteousness of His Son, Jesus Christ, who will be the lamb to be slain to bring restoration to the land. The curse on the land was elevated by the various places on the land where the blood of the Lamb of God touched as He journeyed to the cross and on the cross. As the blood touches the cursed ground, it will liberate it from the curse. His blood touched the soil to liberate it, and as you walk with God, He will liberate you from your sin. The blood of Jesus is the ultimate sacrifice for our freedom, and as you accept Jesus Christ as your Savior, you will be redeemed.

I will make you and the woman hate each other; her offspring and yours will always be enemies. Her offspring will crush your head, and you will bite her offspring's heel (Genesis 3:15).

And the Lord *God made clothes out of animal skins for Adam and his wife, and he clothed them* (Genesis 3:21).

As Jesus said in the Scriptures: The thief comes only in order to steal, kill and destroy. I have come in order that you might have life and life in all its fullness (John 10:10).

Then Jesus went to Nazareth, where he had been brought up, and on the Sabbath He went as usual to the synagogue. He stood up to read the Scriptures and was handed the book of the prophet Isaiah. He unrolled the scroll and found the place where it is written, **"The Spirit of the Lord is upon me, because he has chosen me to bring good news to the poor. He has sent me to proclaim liberty to the captives and recovery of sight to the blind, to set free the oppressed and announce that the time has come when the Lord will save his people."** *Jesus rolled up the scroll, gave it back to the attendant, and sat down. All the people in the synagogue had their eyes fixed on him, as he said to them, "This passage of scripture has come true today, as you heard it being read"* (Emphasis added, Luke 4:16-21).

As Jesus read these Scriptures from the Book of prophet Isaiah and made the proclamation in Luke 4:21, Jesus rose from His seat behind the banquet table, where He had shared bread and wine (representing His flesh and blood) with His disciples (John 1:4-5). He took off His royal robe, tied His serving towel around His waist, and started His work of bringing the Church together as one by sharing the good news to the poor, proclaiming liberty to the captives, giving sight to the blind, setting the oppressed free, and announcing salvation to all.

The introductory book, *The Oneness: Mystery Behind the Construction of the Lampstand*, introduces the reader to the chapters to be treated in this series. It gives brief knowledge of what law is and what it entails. The book looks into the oneness of Genesis 1:1. We do not know what the truth of God's Word is, and Pontius Pilate affirms this when he asked Jesus in John 18:38, "What is the truth?" Likewise, I am asking you to read this book so that your peace will be complete and the truth can be seen. The Lord has asked us to wait patiently and see that He will deliver us from our troubles. Instead, we have turned against Him and worshipped idols such as wealth that we should not be worshipping in the Church. We are just like the Israelites in Exodus 32 who made a bull calf out of melted gold, worshiped and offered sacrifices to it when Moses went up to Mount Sinai to receive the written commandments because they were impatient.

- Why can we not wait for God's promise?

In the last days, simply living life will be difficult and not easy. Waiting on the Lord will be the only option. Wait on the Lord, and He will show you the way to Himself. Wait on the Lord, for the last days are dangerous! The Lord has made His Word available to us and His Word will stand in times of trial. Through the hard times, the Word of the Lord will endeavor pain, which will be short-lived. The Son of God will come in no time, and His coming will be like a thief in the night when no one is aware—when people are sleeping and not keeping watch.

Things will change drastically in this world. The Lord will pull down all strongholds because the power of authority is in His hands, and He will be the One to reign over the earth. All the things I will share in this book series are things yet to come. If you are a follower of Jesus Christ, you will enjoy this book. If, on the other hand, you forfeit your life for the life of the world, then the Lord will permit you to have the pleasures of the world.

The Lord is coming, but He will not tell us when, and when that time comes, He will be in His highest place—kingdom rest, and ask us to join Him. *What are you doing to fulfill God's kingdom rest? What are you fighting against to achieve His kingdom rest?*

Part One

The Word of the Lord

"This book is the record of the events that Jesus Christ revealed. God gave him this revelation in order to show to his servants what must happen very soon. Christ made these things known to his servant John by sending his angel to him, and John has told all that he has seen. This is his report concerning the message from God and the truth revealed by Jesus Christ. Happy is the one who reads this book, and happy are those who listen to the words of this prophetic message and obey what is written in this book! For the time is near when all these things will happen." (Revelation 1:1-3)

Chapter One

To the Church

Those who fight for the Word of God shall endure the pain to the end, but for those who fight for themselves, they shall live for the world and die for the world, while God's people will live forever and ever. Fight for the Lord and you will see who He is. Stay in your faith because it is only your faith that will bring you out of distress. The days are getting shorter and tougher, but the Word of God is with us. Live with it, abide by it, and it shall be well with you. Living in this world is harder than before—living life as the Bible commands is not easy, but the Lord is with His followers.

These days are like the "days of Elijah" where a person's faith was deeply tested by the Lord.

Double portion will be your share if you abide with the Word of God and follow His footsteps (Isaiah 61:7). You will do more than the Lord did because of your obedience. Your portion will be doubled, and you will dwell in His kingdom. The Lord is coming soon to this world of confusion, and His Word will be known to us. We shall abide with His Word, and His Word shall abide with us. He is God, and His promises are forever. He is God, and He will always rescue us. Follow Him with His Word from the east to the west and from the north to the south, and He will care for you in times of difficulty. He will be your rescuer.

In the coming years, life will be even harder than it is now, but the Lord will rescue you from the coming years of hardship. Tough decisions must be made, but the Lord will make Himself known to you through His Word. Then you will decide to which kingdom you want to belong. God will show you His path (which is the path of righteousness) for you to choose.

Man has become a follower of money because of the present hardships in the world, but the Lord offers His perfect peace instead. Chasing after money does not bring peace because money comes and goes; however, the Word of God will always be here with us. And if you know the Word, which is Jesus Christ, your peace would be perfected with God's blessings. This is God's Word—perfect peace!

God sent a message through His servant, John, to the seven churches in the province of Asia about the presentation of His Son, Jesus Christ, the Messiah, who is coming in the latter days. This message is in preparation for what is to come into the world. The world will be full of monsters, and the wild beast is about to come in the same presentation as His Son, Jesus Christ. But the Lord is warning the churches beforehand about the presentation of His Son. The word is that the Son of God and the beast look alike.

- The question is, can you tell the two apart?

To the Seven Churches

From John to the seven churches in the province of Asia: Grace and peace be yours from God, who is, who was, and who is to come, and from the seven spirits in front of his throne, and from Jesus Christ, the faithful witness, the first to be raised from death and who is also the ruler of the kings of the world. He loves us, and by his sacrificial death he has freed us from our sins…" (Revelation 1:4-5).

God has made Himself visible to man because He is a Spirit being. Man lives in this world as a human being, capable of discerning the physical but not the supernatural, and as such, without His revelation, man would never make Him out from among the multitudes. The revelation John gave says in Revelation 1:12 and 13 that *"…I saw seven gold lampstands and among them there was **what looked like a human being**"* (emphasis added)

As a Spirit being, God had to give His attributes to the church in comparison to who we are as humans and how we understand the supernatural. We, as humans, live in the flesh, and our understanding of the supernatural is hindered by our intelligence. Therefore, His interpretation to us of who He is must be done to our level of understanding. He gave us the vision according to our intelligence so that we may know the truth and the signs of who His Son, Jesus Christ, is among us. We should, therefore, work on our understanding of who He is.

He is a Spirit being, and we could never tell Him from the crowd without Him telling us what He looks like. Without the vision or prior warning, we would all be lost in the coming Church. The "truth" of God's Word should be known. He gave us the vision in Revelation 1:9-20 to prepare the Church ahead of time. It was only a vision of who He is as Christ the Savior! God has made it clear that His ways are set and unshaken. He is the "I am that I am," and all of His ways are determined.

He is the One who reigns in us now and will in the future days to come. God is here now with you, but He remains invisible. When He came in the beginning, He came to you in the flesh as a child born to the Virgin Mary, and He will come again in the Spirit to dwell with you in your heart. He will be with you in your heart as He was in the beginning of the world when the Lord breathed life-giving breath into the nostrils of man, making him a living soul. He will be there with you in times of need. God came to you in this world as a Lamb—*humble and fearful*. He will return again as that gentle Lamb in your midst— *fearless and in need*.

God talks about His menorah (the lampstand) in the tabernacle which gives the seven churches equal grace in Exodus 25:31-40.

The Lampstand

The buds, the branches, and the lampstand are to be a single piece of pure hammered gold. Make seven lamps for the lampstand and set them up so that they shine toward the front. Make its tongs and trays of pure gold. Use seventy-five pounds of pure gold to make the lampstand and all this equipment. Take care to make them according to the plan that I showed you on the mountain. (Exodus 25:36-40; GNT).

Hammered is an adjective that means:
- *Shaped or worked with a hammer and often showing hammer marks*

The verb *hammer* means the following:
- *To beat or drive (a nail, peg, etc.) with a hammer*

- *To fasten by using hammer and nails; nail [often fol. by down, up, etc.]*
- *To assemble or build with a hammer and nails [often fol. by together]*
- *To beat out: to hammer brass*
- *To form or construct by repeated, vigorous, or strenuous effort [often fol. by out or together]*
- *To pound or hit forcefully*

The lampstand, which is one of the furniture in the tabernacle (*means: tent, place of dwelling or sanctuary*), was constructed under specific instructions by God to Moses at Mount Sinai. A tabernacle is a sanctuary pitched in the wilderness. After coming out of the Egyptian slavery (Exodus 12–15: 21), God through Moses instructed the Israelites to pitch Him a sanctuary (a portable church) in the wilderness as they journeyed through it until their victory over the occupants of the Promised Land, where He will meet them. Every time the people of Israel set up a camp, Moses pitches "this church" some distance away from the camp. Why, because at the camp are some who still have beliefs in the gods of the Egyptians.

Then have them make a sanctuary for me, and I will dwell among them. Make this tabernacle and all its furnishings exactly like the pattern I will show you. - (Exodus 25:8-9)

Whenever the people of Israel set up camp, Moses would take the sacred Tent and put it up some distance outside the camp. It was called the Tent of the Lord's presence, and anyone who wanted to consult the Lord would go out to it. - (Exodus 33:7)

The purpose of the lampstand in the tabernacle is to bring light (illumination) to God's people. It has this purpose because that is what God made of it—to bring light to His people in darkness. His people have been blinded by their circumstances and pain. God promised them a land flowing with milk and honey—freedom, but His people still felt bounded and desperate. Their situation is worse than when they were in slavery and they are meant to be free. They are lost and losing faith and desperate. We might be free, but still feel in bondage. How do we believe in this light God has given us in this wilderness, when all we see is doom? That is the vision of the Lord—illumination. God brought illumination to the world of darkness where no light shines. He discriminated the enemy and brought light. Jesus is the light to this darkened world; the light born to bring us out of darkness—*the darkness of this age.*

Jesus spoke to the Pharisees again. "I am the light of the world," he said. "Whoever follows me will have the light of life and will never walk in darkness. – (John 8:12)

I have come into the world as light, so that everyone who believes in me should not remain in the darkness. – (John 12:46)

The purpose of the lampstand in the holy place is to bring memory to the Israelites about their journey through the Red Sea and the wilderness. God did not ask them to build Him a tabernacle when they were in Egypt, but He did so when they left Egypt because they needed Him to be with them and a reminder of who He is—a physical presentation of Him and His promise.

He asked them to build Him a tabernacle so that He will dwell among them. When they were in Egypt, they were in bondage to the law of the land which did not favor them. God could not ask them to build Him a temple until He brought them out of that bondage. They were in bondage to a faith they did not understand, and as they came out of that bondage, their minds were freed to think otherwise. They had the liberty to reach out to their faith.

Therefore, the tabernacle was placed a good distance away from the camp, where the Israelites who want to seek God would do so outside the camp. In the camp are:

- Complication of faith
- Faithless people
- People still carrying the gods of the Egyptians

The Israelites came out of Egypt with the Egyptian gods; therefore, they lived in the wilderness, a place of dryness. The lampstand is the place where God meets His people and the place where we perceive His will. It represents who you are in the Lord and where you are regarding His law. It tells you to which Church you belong based on your position with His Word and modifies your understanding concerning the things of God.

It is a special place in the Lord where He lays down His rules for the Church, which is where all the rules are set. These established rules will constitute the coming of the Lord in the last days. His kingdom will be judged on these set rules. You should not live on bread alone but on every spoken word of the Lord. You should have faith in Him.

Then the Spirit led Jesus into the desert to be tempted by the devil. After spending forty days and nights without food, Jesus was hungry. Then the devil came to him and said, if you are God's Son, order these stones to turn into bread. But Jesus answered, the scripture says, Human beings cannot live on bread alone, but need every word that God speaks (Matthew 4:4).

…He loves us, and by his sacrificial death He has freed us from our sins and made us a kingdom of priests to serve His God and Father. To Jesus Christ be the glory and power forever and ever! Amen (Revelation 1:5-6).

This Scripture speaks of the kingdom of saints being awakened at the end of this world in order to serve the Lord in His kingdom. We are preserved for God's worship in the end. You are His anointed saints who will stay in faith until the end of the struggle. These are the struggles of preparing the priests in His convent, the Holy Place.

Look, He is coming on the clouds! Everyone will see Him, including those who pierced Him. All people on earth will mourn over Him. So shall it be! I am the first and the last, says the Lord God Almighty, who is, who was, and who is to come (Revelation 1:7).

The Church of God is coming! He has already given us the description of the Church in John's vision of Christ and has prepared the Church by the beating of the pure gold into the lampstand in preparation for His Church to come. Look at things carefully because the world is changing very fast. People's rights will be defended, and the Church will be in no place but to adjust to these demands of the world. The Church will bend its rules in favor of the world.

These changes will affect man, and man will have nowhere to turn but will be forced to adhere to these changes. The world will be a living hell, and the Church will follow suit. Woe to anyone who listens to the world's system; they will live in a very dry place because the love of God will not be with them. The Church shall live in the desert because God will dissociate Himself from the people. Their lives will be cut short because they are in breach of God's will. They have disrespected God in His land. God will leave them to burn in hell—the very world that they have created for themselves.

The seasons are changing and they can be seen from the way things are happening in the world today. What we think as the end of this world, is actually the beginning of God's kingdom. God is putting things in place through our hardship. The deliverer is coming! The days about which Isaiah spoke in the Bible (Isaiah 7:17-25) are about to manifest. These days are dangerous and frightening.

I shall live my days according to the word of God. I feel this anguish in my heart as I write this message because the Lord is revealing so much to me, and the sight of what I am seeing brings fear and anguish.

• How shall we live and survive these coming days about which the Lord is talking?

We will need strong faith in our hearts to sustain us in this world. Our faith as children of God will be tested.

We will need God's love in our hearts to survive the hardship, and that love is Jesus Christ. Without that love, we will fail the Lord and end up in the furnace with the rest. The Lord is coming soon. Prepare your heart for Him because He is the only One who can help you survive that season. You need Jesus Christ in your life because the days are dangerous. We need to live by Christ alone. We need to worship God and Him alone. Watch out for the Popes; they are going to change the world!

The mourner (Matthew 5:4) who lives under God's Tent of the Lord's presence will see His awesome glory when He comes. God will show Himself to you. He paid a huge price on your behalf by suffering humiliation and death on the cross. Those who pierced Him will see Him as their Lord and Savior. He will announce His coming to all, and you shall see Him come as He rides in His glory. God shall make His will known to you.

He gave us the vision of the One to save us. He forewarned the churches of the coming of Satan, the beast, into this world and His churches. But be warned, the Devil is no respecter of faith. He will make his way into the Church and destroy all that you believe in. He will trample over your beliefs. He will change your belief system (rules and regulations) in the Church.

Satan is bringing division among the churches. We should know who Christ is among the churches; therefore, God gave us the vision of Christ as the child who is yet to be given as a son. He has been birthed to us as a child, but yet to be given as a son. God gave us a vision of His Son for reference purposes as the beast enters the churches.

Chapter Two

A Vision of Christ

I am John, your brother, and as a follower of Jesus I am your partner in patiently enduring the suffering that comes to those who belong to His Kingdom. <u>I was put on the island of Patmos</u> because I had proclaimed God's word and the truth that Jesus revealed. <u>On the Lord's day</u> the Spirit took control of me, and I heard a loud voice, that sounded like a trumpet, <u>speaking behind me</u>. It said, write down what you see, and send the book to the churches in these seven cities: Ephesus, Smyrna, Pergamum, Thyatira, Sardis, Philadelphia, and Laodicea (Revelation 1:9).

The island of Patmos is a place where you proclaim your destiny—a place where God's word is revealed to you. Patmos was a rocky and barren island in the Aegean Sea. John, the disciple of Jesus, was banished to this island during the latter years of his life. He was placed there because he had come to a point in his journey with God where God's vision had to be made clear to him. He was placed there for a purpose to witness the coming of the Church.

The Vision

John started his letter by saying, *"as a follower of Jesus, I am your partner in patiently enduring the suffering that comes to those who belong to His Kingdom."* He was banished to that island because of his purpose—proclaiming the truth of God's word. Although we do find suffering as unjust, sometimes it is the very way of bringing us to our destiny. Our purpose is unleashed through sufferings.

Sometimes, like John, you need to withdraw from certain crowds or environments to achieve your destiny. You need to be placed in the hands of the right people who will bring you into your destiny one way or another. You will need to lay down your heart for God and no one else.

John's destiny came to him when he was placed in the right place. There, God made Himself visible to him. He was shown the truth of God's word, Jesus Christ, the Deliverer. A vision was given behind the human flesh. What will those who claim to be God's choice simply because of their race say to God now? God is speaking to John outside his human flesh—a concept that no one understands except God Himself. He does not look at a person's race though He understands every race, and He does not differentiate between races because He created them all. Otherwise, He will be calling or referring to Himself as unfaithful or a liar.

God called John and spoke to him in the spirit. He called him out of his human flesh and spoke with the spirit that dwelt in John—the same life-giving breath that God breathed into the nostrils of man in Genesis 2:7. Differentiation is not possible here because God cannot and will not differentiate Himself from us. He created man in His image. We are a presentation of Him on earth. So, for all who think they are superior to others, I have some bad news for you. God is God and will always remain God regardless of your thoughts.

- *Have you read the end of the Bible yet?*

The Word of the Lord says the following:

"I, John, solemnly warn everyone who hears the prophetic words of this book: if any add anything to them, God will add to their punishment the plagues described in this book. And if any take anything away from the prophetic words of this book, God will take away from them their share of the fruit of the tree of life and of the Holy City, which are described in this book. He who gives his testimony to all this says, "Yes indeed! I am coming soon!" So be it. Come, Lord Jesus! May the grace of the Lord

Jesus be with underline{everyone}" (Emphasis added, Revelation 22:18-21).

John had no distractions from the world because he was in exile and out of reach of people. God made Himself known visibly to John in the Spirit. John had to be in the Spirit to be able to see and understand God's will. He had to be in the Spirit to understand God, so the Lord had to bring him back to who he was before he was born—as a spirit man (Jeremiah 1:5). That is why he had to turn back to his former state to listen and hear what the Lord was saying because God is a Spirit being (John 4:24). There is a level of worship that brings us to this realm of the spirit.

He could not have done it in the flesh; therefore, he had to be in the Spirit to listen to the voice that created him. In the spirit realm, John was able to see the Lord, listen to Him and understand His word. In our human form, many things distract us and keep us away from God's word and revelations. John made it in the Spirit where he was not distracted. This is the place where God brings you in order to get your attention to give you His message and proclaim His will. God speaks to your spirit. John had to be translated from the fleshly realm to the spirit realm to be able to listen to and understand God's will. In the spirit realm, the child of God can achieve a great deal.

The vision of Christ is a warning in the Bible to go out to the churches about who God is among His people. This warning has been given to the churches as to what is to come in the days ahead. The great monster has been released and is heading toward the churches—the seven churches that lie within Christ. Be aware of the warning and gird up your loins because the Word of God is going to be thrown into chaos. The Word of the Lord is going to go through a tremendous test.

The whole world's culture will be tested by the Enemy, but the Word of the Lord will always stand. This is simply a revelation of what Christ looks like. A vision received by Moses (Exodus 33:19-23) and re-imposed on John—The Vision. John received the same vision of Christ. You will need the grace of God to help you differentiate between Him and the accuser of the brethren (Revelation 12:10).

The great monster is not as horrible looking as the world has taught us to believe. He comes as a carbon copy image of Jesus Christ, the Deliverer. He comes as a counterfeit image of Christ, therefore his easy access to the Church. Be careful who you let into your church and into your space, they may be a wolf in a sheep's skin. The Devil is aimlessly wandering around <u>like</u> a roaring lion, but Jesus is the authentic Lion of the tribe of Judah (Revelation 5:5).

Be alert, be on watch! Your enemy, the Devil, roams around like a roaring lion, looking for someone to devour. Be firm in your faith and resist him, because you know that other believers in all the world are going through the same kind of sufferings. (1 Peter 5:8-9)

The Church will be deceived into believing in the great monster, therefore the reason for the vision of Christ before His coming.

- Christ is coming, but who is He?

Watch out in your pews!

The great monster has been released into the world. The principles of the Church are going to change. There will be hardship in this world of darkness. The Lord says you're to put His Word in your heart and live by it. Living in the world will be difficult; it will interfere with your principles and beliefs, but the Lord has made provision for these days.

The concept of God's sacrifice is not understood because He gave us His all, the very image of Himself to be sacrificed and rescue us from the hands of the enemy. Such a gesture is a total sacrifice. He will lead us out of Egypt, our land of slavery, take us through our wilderness of shame to the land promised to us—Canaan. God will bring us out in His name as He has promised, but in our wilderness, we walk around in circles in our disbelief without achieving anything, till we believe. It is an image to view.

He has given us His all, all in the name of salvation to bring us out of hardship. Just as He brought the Hebrews out of Egypt, so will He bring us out of the slavery which we find ourselves in through the worship of other gods. He will do just as He has promised. It is an image to view.

He gave His all, in the name of salvation to bring us out of hardship and darkness. He will bring us to fruition and light.

God has given us His Son to bring us out of this shame and struggle. His Son will be our Deliverer, and He will bring us into the world that the Father has already prepared for those of His children who will fight until the end.

The End of Days Are Here!

God has just given us the image of His Son, Jesus Christ, the Savior of this world. It is left with us to find who this Son is. Search within yourself and the churches for the sign of Christ within them. The vision is only a portrait of Christ—what He looks like—not who He is. To know who He really is, you will have to search within yourself. God, in His infinite self, will make Him available to you. He is the Lord your God, who has come to His own.

The vision tells us that God is among us (the lampstand with seven branches), and His main purpose is to bring us (salvation) out of this dark world into the world of the Lord by the process of illumination. Jesus is the bridge between God and man, bringing us together with God (restoration). He also aligns with God's Word. After all, only God's principles will stand in the end.

The Image of Christ

I turned around to see who was talking to me, and I saw seven gold lampstands, and among them was what looked like a human being, wearing a robe that reached to his feet, and a gold band around his chest. His hair was white as wool, or as snow, and his eyes blazed like fire; his feet shone like brass that has been refined and polished, and his voice sounded like a roaring waterfall. He held seven stars in his right hand, and a sharp two-edged sword came out of his mouth. His face was as bright as the midday sun. When I saw him, I fell down at his feet like a dead man. He placed his right hand on me and said, Don't be afraid! I am the first and the last. I am the living one! I was dead, but now I am alive forever and ever. I have authority over death and the world of the dead. Write, then, the things you see, both the things that are now and the things that will happen afterward. Here is the secret meaning of the seven stars that you see in my right hand, and of the seven gold lampstands: the seven stars are the angels of the seven churches, and the seven lampstands are the seven churches. (Revelation 1:12-20)

God revealed to John the image of Christ and requested of him to send the message to the seven churches about whom Christ is, as well as His appearance and what He possesses. In His right hand is the seven stars—the angels to the churches. This Scripture reveals what Christ looks like in the Church. Among the seven lampstands, this is what Christ looks like. These are the principles birthed to you in the churches. Anything outside these principles is birthed by Satan. They are the works of the Enemy, so take note of who Christ is among you—the One for whom the alabaster box was broken—*the perfume* (Matthew 26:7).

He wears a gold band around His chest. It is a banner of who He is, the liberator of man. Does the gold band differentiate between Christ and the beast? The beast cannot make gold out of its nature, but it borrows the nature of man.

Christ is the One you should follow, because in your time of distress, many people will appear to the churches as being the Savior. Satan is on the rampage. For you to know who the true Savior is, God had to reveal Himself in the spirit to John for him to pass on the message of who he saw to his brethren. This was done in case someone passes himself off as the Savior of this world. With the knowledge you possess, you would be able to tell Christ from the crowd. Let me introduce you to Christ!

John saw the following:
- Seven gold lampstands
- Among them was a figure like a human being
- Wearing a robe that reached to His feet
- A gold belt round His chest
- His hair was white as wool or snow
- His eyes blazed like fire

- His feet shone like brass that has been refined and polished
- His voice sounded like a roaring waterfall
- He held seven stars in His right hand
- A sharp two-edged sword came out of His mouth
- His face was as bright as the midday sun

John's message describes Christ as a "figure" that looked like a human being. A *figure* as a noun meaning includes:
- *Visible shape or form; the outline*
- *A pictorial or sculptural representation, especially of the human body*
- *A person as impressed on the mind*

The Sign of Hope

Then the Lord said, "There is a place near me where you may stand on a rock. When my glory passes by, I will put you in a cleft in the rock and cover you with my hand until I have passed by. Then I will remove my hand and you will see my back; but my face must not be seen." (Exodus 33:21-23)

The sign of hope—the LORD said to Moses, "There is A PLACE near me where you may stand on A ROCK. The sign that justifies our salvation and in that sign is our hope." He has a place near Him where we may stand on a rock to see His glory—the rock of our salvation.

- What is this place near Him?

In that place is a rock where we may stand on, and as His glory passes by, He will hide us in the cleft (a usually narrow partial opening caused by splitting and rupture) of the rock and cover us with His hand. There is a place in the LORD where all our troubles are laid before Him, and He gives us hope that all will be well. Even amid worries, He gives us hope in that place. That place is Jesus Christ.

As you journey to the place of Christ, He will take on all your troubles and give you peace within. He will show you the path to Him. Christ is the place where all our hope should be. God places us in Him so that His glory will shine on us as He passes by. The splendor of the LORD is with us, even in our deep sorrow. He is with us, regardless. The rock of our salvation!

In Exodus 33:18-23, Moses asked the LORD to show him His glory. God answered him that He would cause all of His Glory to pass in front of him and proclaim His name, the LORD, to him. God agreed to show Moses His glory, but first, He placed him in a place near Him, and in that place was a rock which he stood on. When His glory passed by, God hid Moses in the cleft of the rock and covered him with His hand till He passed. He removed His hand after for Moses to see His back, as no one lives after seeing His face.

There is a place in God where we all have to be. A place where we will stand on a rock to see all of His glory passes. There is a place in God where all our worries sit, and this place is in Jesus Christ. He is the rock of our salvation. In Him is life, and in Him is our salvation. As His glory passes by, He hides us in the wounds of the Lord Jesus Christ and covers us with His mighty Hand. God protects us from the wrath of the enemy. He plants us in Christ for our salvation.

I am scared if I am strong enough to stay put in this place. As I write this text, I feel this anguish and fear in my heart, that I may not be able to meet my side of the bargain. I am scared of what is required of me to do so. I feel it's not possible considering the world we live in and the fallen nature of man.

- Would I be able to live outside the world's demands?
- How can I be in the world and not love the things of the world (1 John 2:15-17; John 17:6-9)?

That is our weakness—being in the world and not loving the things of the world. How do we live such a life?

But the answer lies in the Word of God. The solution to our problem lies in His Son, Jesus Christ—the Redeemer of our faith. He has come to teach and show us the way to God. He has set His rules, and the journey is tedious. We have to live by His example.

We do not know the "how," but He has been born to show us—Jesus is the Way, the Truth, and the Life (John 14:6). He is the Living God among His people, therefore, it is important to live by His principles—the Sermon on the Mount.

To establish our greatness, we have to live by His principles (Matthew 5-7). Building the Kingdom of God is where Jesus comes in, to create greatness in us. To fellowship with God is a great desire, but to follow His principles needs the grace of God, which is Christ our Lord. The desire to worship God lies in our faith, but we are on the brink of our faith.

I have to look up to the cross at Calvary, the stripes on Jesus' back, and His sufferings to enjoy God's promises. The same back was seen by Moses when the goodness of God passed by him to show His Glory. Moses only saw His back. God hid the link (Moses; *the Covenant made*) to His Promise in the cleft of the rock, and that rock is the Son of God. In Him is the Covenant to the Promised Land. In Him lives the Covenant of God.

Jesus is the rock on which Moses stood and was hidden in its cleft as God showed him all of His goodness. He invested His word in Jesus. As the goodness of God passes through this land, His faithful children will see the back of His Glory, in the same way as Jesus walked the Earth. Jesus passed by, traveling through the Earth, leaving His marks and picking up our marks on His back. And at the end of His journey, all we can see are the wounds on His back acquired for our sake.

In those wounds are our healing—by the stripes of Jesus, we are healed. In those stripes is the resurrection of our faith. Jesus showed us the back of God that Moses saw when He showed him all of His goodness. Moses walked the path that God walked and saw His goodness. He descended from the mountain after spending forty days and nights in the presence of God with the reflection of His Glory on his face (Exodus 34:29-32).

> *I love you, Lord, my strength. The Lord is my rock, my fortress, and my deliverer; my God is my rock, in whom I take refuge, my shield, and the horn of my salvation, my stronghold.* (Psalm 18:1-2)

These are part of the words that David, the servant of the LORD, sang to God when He delivered him from the hand of all his enemies and that of Saul. Let's remember:

- In the promises of God is His salvation!
- If I am to see the glory of God, then I have to place myself in Jesus Christ and stand on His Word.
- Worship and serve Him alone as my God!

Chapter Three

Seven Golden Lampstands

The seven golden lampstands represent the seven churches in equal division. God shares among them an equal anointing and judgment. He is the lampstands in the Holy Place that provides illumination. He is the light of the lampstands. Jesus is the light in the Holy Place. He provides the same anointing in any other church; therefore, His presence is with all at equal times. God will provide love in our church because He is love. He stands among His people and becomes their Provider—Jehovah Jireh. He supplies their needs according to His riches in glory.

The Lampstands

Jesus was describing the Faithful Church to John because it is the last to come. Describing the Faithful Church in a human form is the mystery to the vision. That is why He stood among the seven churches and did not describe it as human but as the Church to come in the days of strife. It is God's Faithful Church dressed in a robe that reaches to His feet—the royal robe. This is how He instructed the Hebrews to construct the outer covering of His tabernacle.

The New Jerusalem

One of the seven angels who had the seven bowls full of the seven last plagues came to me and said, "Come, and I will show you the Bride, the wife of the Lamb." The Spirit took control of me, and the angel carried me to the top of a very high mountain. He showed me Jerusalem, the Holy City, coming down out of heaven from God and shining with the glory of God. The city shone like a precious stone, like a jasper, clear as crystal. It had a great, high wall with twelve gates and with twelve angels in charge of the gates. On the gates were written the names of the twelve tribes of the people of Israel. There were three gates on each side: three on the east, three on the south, three on the north, and three on the west. The city's wall was built on twelve foundation stones, on which were written the names of the twelve apostles of the Lamb. The angel who spoke to me had a gold measuring stick to measure the city, its gates, and its wall. The city was perfectly square, as wide as it was long. The angel measured the city with his measuring stick: it was fifteen hundred miles long and was as wide and as high as it was long. The angel also measured the wall, and it was 216 feet high, according to the standard unit of measure which he was using. The wall was made of jasper, and the city itself was made of pure gold, as clear as glass. The foundation stones of the city wall were adorned with all kinds of precious stones. The first foundation stone was jasper, the second sapphire, the third agate, the fourth emerald, the fifth onyx, the sixth carnelian, the seventh yellow quartz, the eighth beryl, the ninth topaz, the tenth chalcedony, the eleventh turquoise, the twelfth amethyst. The twelve gates were twelve pearls; each gate was made from a single pearl. The street of the city was of pure gold, transparent as glass.

I did not see a temple in the city, because its temple is the Lord God Almighty and the Lamb. The city has no need of the sun or the moon to shine on it, because the glory of God shines on it, and the Lamb is its lamp. The peoples of the world will walk by its light, and the kings of the earth will bring their wealth into it. The gates of the city will stand open all day; they will never be closed, because there will be no night there. The greatness and the wealth of the nations will be brought into the city. But nothing that is impure will enter the city, nor anyone who does shameful things or tells lies. Only those whose names are written in the Lamb's book of the living will enter the city (Revelation 21:9-27).

The Faithful Church comes with a gold belt around its chest, which corresponds with the return of Jesus Christ to this world. He stands among the seven golden lampstands. This is the message of the vision. John described His outer covering—His divinity, the entrance to the tabernacle (which is His brass feet), the inner sanctuary, and the laws of the Lord (the two-edged sword). The convocation of the Lord!

The word *convocation* means the following:

- *A formal assembly at a college or university, esp. for a graduation ceremony.*
- *A group gathered in response to a summons*
- *An assembly of the clergy of part of a diocese in the Episcopal church*

Revelation 1:17-18

When I saw him, I fell down at his feet like a dead man. He placed his right hand on me and said, don't be afraid! I am the first and the last. I am the living one! I was dead, but now I am alive forever and ever. I have authority over death and the world of the dead.

This scripture reflects on the story of the two disciples who were sent to witness the empty tomb of Jesus (John 20:1-10).

John's experience of the empty tomb has been narrated in the verses of Revelation 1:17-18. Both disciples went on the same journey with one destination, but the route and time taken to get there were different.

John took a different route but met Jesus, the resurrected Christ, and upon seeing His awesomeness, fell at His feet and offered himself to the Lord to use him at His will. John believed and surrendered his life to Him. Jesus became His Shepherd, and John became the Lord's sheep. God placed His hand of authority on His disciple and ushered him into His kingdom. God placed His authority on John through the Pentecostal fire baptism (Acts 2:1-4), which consumed him with the love of God and ushered him into the world.

Revelation 1:19-20
Write, then, the things you see, both the things that are now and the things that will happen afterward. Here is the secret meaning of the seven stars that you see in my right hand, and of the seven gold lampstands: the seven stars are the angels of the seven churches, and the seven lampstands are the seven churches.

John was given the authority to write and pass the message on to the seven churches of the province of Asia that which he had witnessed when he leaned over to look inside the tomb (John 20:1-18) and what he saw when he finally stepped into the empty tomb. Both are different; (1) *to lean over to look* inside the empty tomb gives an answer to a question and (2), *entering the empty tomb* removes doubt.

Until John entered the tomb, he did not understand the Word that has been given to him—Jesus. John witnessed the truth of God's Word through the vision. The Word was given to him as a figure that looked like a human being—it only looked like a human being, but not a human being.

The vision gave him what the Word looks like in the sight of his eyes. Christ gave John the image of Him in the presence of Himself, meaning Christ is within us and our understanding of who He is lies within us. He is Christ in the Church and Jehovah Jireh in us.

The principles of the Church are simple, but the theory of who Christ is to us is complicated, considering Him living in us. We are Christ, and He is us. The theory of the love He has for us is amazing and at the same time complicated. He died on the cross in our place as He bore our sins on Him to the cross and carried them to the grave. He resurrected with no shame on Him. He rid us of our sins and loved us. He is our pride and shame.

Christ died for us to be free of our sins and shame. He is our resurrection. We live in Him, and Him in us (1 John 4:13).

The six gold branches extending from the sides of the golden lampstands indicate that the Lord God had His mission in place when He set up the churches. The church that lies in the middle (shaft) of the lampstands feeds the six branches with His grace and mercy. Although these branches (churches) lie within the grace of God, they have to meet a certain standard for them to be called the sons of God. The vision of Christ is preaching about the standards needed to be met in the name of Jesus to achieve His principles. The messages of God go out in a time of need for the Church to build up on their difference and character. Also, there is the need to reach out to people as the Lord reached out to them in the lampstand by constantly supplying them with grace and understanding.

The lampstand is to bring peace extending from it to the churches and show the path to God. God did not bring it to punish the Church but in a way to set the path for them as a rescue plan to His kingdom of peace. So, the shaft feeding all the six branches represents the Faithful Church. This is very complicated because the Lord has designed the lampstand in a way that will demonstrate who He is in the kingdom of God. He is the supplier of our faith in terms of socialization.

God gives us our strength to carry on and reveals to us the prototype of His plan.

- Who is He to us because He only showed Moses the image of His back?

He has planted in us what needs to be made right in achieving His goal, but this is far-fetched if we keep going around in circles instead of achieving what He intends for us to achieve. The plan of God for mankind is simple—to achieve His goal of prosperity, i.e., achieving everything that He has set before us in time immemorial.

He has set His desires before us in achieving His will on earth, and until that happens, we will forever lack the things of God (His grace, wisdom, knowledge, and admiration) in the Church. He has set the menorah and has given us the vision of His perfect Church—the faith-ridden Church of the Lord.

• Now, how shall we bring ourselves to the point where all we do is Kingdom building, and nothing else?

We have to set standards in the Church to bring us to that position. Setting up that standard is what He has given us in the message to the churches. The Bible tells us what to do to bring ourselves to that position. In other words, bring your church to the standard of the Church that lies in the middle of the lampstand.

The lampstand in the holy place of the tabernacle gives us a picture of who we are in the Lord and what our standards are in comparison to the laws of the Lord. So, we have a lampstand that houses all of the churches in the land and a principle that guards it.

• What shall we do to achieve these standards?

The model that God created was very simple to understand: a lampstand with six branches branching out of it. Therefore, God is grafting the six branches to the shaft of the lampstand—*grafting His churches into one*—although they seem to be a distance apart or at different points and sides of the lampstand.

The churches are attached to the shaft at different positions with distance apart just as the crowd (including His disciples and the women) were when Jesus Christ of Nazareth was on the cross at Calvary. They observed His suffering and death on the cross from a distance—*different positions from the place of the cross*, although they were one with Him and shared their grief as they beat their chest (Luke 23:48) at the revelation of who Jesus is. The crowd was at different positions around the cross, and all looked on to Christ as He died on the cross—*sacrifice*.

The distance as you see it, does not make any difference as the crowd are all grafted to His cross. The branches of the lampstand are all not extending from the same points or sides; some extend from the same side but at different positions. We all don't share the same views, but we do have the same belief in God.

The vision of Christ and the model of the Tent of His presence (the tabernacle) is the purpose of God—the perfect Church to come with the true incense of worship.

The Beating of the Pure Gold

There is to be one bud below each of the three pairs of branches." The buds, the branches, and the lampstand are to be a single piece of pure hammered gold (Exodus 25:35).

The pure gold is to be hammered into one single piece, which pictures how the Church is to be beaten down to form the Perfect Church that the Lord God wants from this gold. The bud bridges the branches and the shaft of the lampstand. The Church is to be worked on in order to bring forth the Perfect Church required by hammering it down to create the one Church needed without tearing it apart. They are to be formed through unison—not division. That is the oneness in God—all things working together for those who love the Lord.

We know that in all things God works for good with those who love him, those whom he has called according to his purpose (Romans 8:28).

The pure gold metal is hammered into shape as ordained by God through the instructions He gave to Moses. The pure gold metal is hammered into shape with Christ in mind. The base and the shaft were hammered out first with its decorative flowers as a single piece, then the six branches with their decorative flowers and then the seven lamps for the lampstand. This shows the sacrifice of Christ before the resurrection of man. Christ was hammered out first, then the churches which lie within the province of Asia.

Christ carried the cross to Calvary and man suffered watching Him die on the cross. Crushing Christ was for the work of the cross. The beating of the pure gold to bring the

Church into shape is actually the building of God's Church to come to pass. He is illustrating how His Church would be built upon His Word—the principles of the Church. He hammered the gold metal until it fitted together as one unit with the shaft of the lamp. Hammering the gold metal is what the Church classifies as dissociation because you feel separated from the will of the world. This process of dissociation takes place in the Church through sacrifice. The Church sacrifices itself for the Word of God. It is beaten down by the Word of God until it matures to become part of the big picture. Therefore, the sacrifice that is made in establishing this is a sacrifice with which to be reckoned.

The churches will be hammered until they are right with God. Thus, you will begin to see the churches experiencing massive changes. The Church must remain strong because, in the long term, these changes are good. The change will be a long-time coming, but this change will affect the way Church operates. This change is long overdue. God will hammer the churches until they change their ways to His ways and fit into His Faithful Church.

John sent the messages to the churches in the right season because grafting depends on time as well. The time of season affects the grafting of a plant. The messages were delivered at the right time to the corresponding churches. The churches were alerted, and the messages were given out. The messages went out to the churches in time for its hammering.

For the seven golden lampstands to be established, the word has to go out to His chosen churches; in other words, the messages to the seven churches in the province of Asia. Christ has given the revealed word according to the need of the Church. God created His word to the churches to bring them to unity. Although God commanded the lampstand to be constructed through the hammering of the pure gold, the message has to be sent to the corresponding churches to bring about the construction. So, He created the messages to the seven churches in the province of Asia according to their needs.

These are the messages that will crush the Church to press out the best olive oil in them, so that they can be favored and also lighten up the lampstand in the holy place. The message is to bring about the hammering. The hammering is the basic job, but the anointing is what will keep the lamp lit from evening until morning.

Therefore, crushing is vital in the process of the hammering. A figure that looked like a human being—*Jesus Christ*—stands among the churches to bring them enlightenment. To make it feasible to construct the oneness of the lampstand, Christ had to die on the cross to bring out our salvation. Therefore, the first parts to be hammered out are the base and the shaft.

The lampstand stands in the holy place as a representation of who Christ is in our midst and what God's idea of unity is. God cannot change His word or go back on His word. What He has spoken, has been spoken. The lampstand is the presence of God in the Church. It represents the One who bore our sins on the cross and brought us retribution. He is God in the form of man. Let us celebrate the Lord in raising His banner high to the world and bring solidarity (meaning: *unity of purpose or interest*) to the world. He is Christ in the Church, and among us is His presence. The lamp has to be lit every evening.

Taking Care of the Lamp

"Command the people of Israel to bring you the best olive oil for the lamp, so that it can be lit each evening. Aaron and his sons are to set up the lamp in the Tent of my presence outside the curtain which is in front of the Covenant Box. There in my presence it is to burn from evening until morning. This command is to be kept forever by the Israelites and their descendants (Exodus 27:20-21).

God hammered the pure gold for our purpose—to bring us out of our distress. The hammered gold is to bring the church together in the name of Jesus. On each lamp is a light that directs its path. These lights together shine up the holy place. A light shines out of each seven churches. The light bowls are the last parts to be constructed and mark the beginning of enlightenment. The Lord embraced our beginning of life with a light.

God commanded the people of Israel to bring the best olive oil (*beaten olives to a degree to show its level of purity*) to lit the lamp every evening. The Church is to bring God the best worship in His sanctuary to light up the lamp.

Part Two

The Hammering

"Make a lampstand of pure gold. Make its base and its shaft of hammered gold; its decorative flowers, including buds and petals, are to form one piece with it."
\- Exodus 25:31

Chapter Four

Grafting

You Gentiles by birth—called "the uncircumcised" by the Jews, who call themselves the circumcised (which refers to what men do to their bodies)—remember what you were in the past. At that time you were apart from Christ. You were foreigners and did not belong to God's chosen people. You had no part in the covenants, which were based on God's promises to his people, and you lived in this world without hope and without God. But now, in union with Christ Jesus you, who used to be far away, have been brought near by the blood of Christ (Ephesians 2:11-13).

The instructions for the construction of the lampstand were all about God's oneness of the Church. This process is to bring these churches into one with the faithful Church. The instructions given were all about oneness for the purpose of creating the universe in Genesis 1. In Exodus 25:31-40, God included the details—the instructions, directions, and process for construction, and within them are the processes of grafting and budding.

The Lampstand

"Make a lampstand of pure gold. Make its base and its shaft of hammered gold; its decorative flowers, including buds and petals, are to form one piece with it. Six branches shall extend from its sides, three from each side. Each of the six branches is to have three decorative flowers shaped like almond blossoms with buds and petals. The shaft of the lampstand is to have four decorative flowers shaped like almond blossoms with buds and petals. There is to be one bud below each of the three pairs of branches. The buds, the branches, and the lampstand are to be a single piece of pure hammered gold. Make seven lamps for the lampstand and set them up so that they shine toward the front. Make its tongs and trays of pure gold. Use seventy-five pounds of pure gold to make the lampstand and all this equipment. Take care to make them according to the plan that I showed you on the mountain. (Exodus 25:31-40)

Grafting and Budding

The meaning of Grafting includes:

- *to cause to grow together parts from different plants, i.e., "graft the cherry tree branch onto the plum tree"*
- *to place the organ of a donor into the body of a recipient*
- *(Horticulture) a piece of plant tissue (the scion), normally a stem, that is made to unite with an established plant (the stock), which supports and nourishes it*
- *(Surgery) Surgically transplanting a piece of tissue or an organ from a donor or from the patient's own body to an area of the body in need of the tissue*

In the formation of oneness, both grafting and budding are present. The six branches are seen grafted to the shaft of the lampstand and with a bud at the place of each branch, joining both parts together. The process of grafting and budding secures a better plant. See Romans 11:16-24; Ephesians 2:11-13, 19; Ephesians 3:6.

Grafting and budding are horticultural techniques used in the industry to connect parts from two or more different plants so that they appear to grow as one. In grafting, the upper part (scion) of one plant grows on the root system (rootstock) of another plant. Whereas, in budding, a bud is taken from one plant and grown on another. The scion becomes a permanent part of the tree over time.

The scion (Church) grows to become the shooting system (with buds, leaves, stems, flowers, and fruits) of the Faithful Church above the ground. The Church does the bonding.

The rootstock (Jesus Christ) extends underground to become the root system that feeds and supports the shooting system.

The graft union is the edge in Jesus' garment where the woman with the issue of blood touched and got healed. It stands for the bond between them and brings the Church together with Christ.

The advantages of grafting include combining attributes that do not naturally occur in a single plant. The new plant that grows from the scion will be exactly like the plant from which it came. The purpose of grafting is to improve the attributes of the plants. The rootstock plant is the plant that provides a root system and base, which in the case of the lampstand, is the shaft and the base. Both were hammered out first. The point where the two parts connect (the branch to the shaft) is secured and protected with a bud.

The Branches

The branches of the lampstand include us. God left no one out, but if we refuse to listen or heed to His word, He will branch us out as He did with the natural branch in Romans 11:17. We are the six branches of the lampstand. These branches stand for those who live in Christ and Christ in them. The branches are for us to belong. The branches are six but the main root is one. You cannot have the branch without the root. The branches are the different churches in the Lord. They look structurally alike, but are spiritually different. They feed into the shaft of the lampstand, but their nutritional needs are different from each other.

I am the real vine, and my Father is the gardener. He breaks off every branch in me that does not bear fruit, and he prunes every branch that does bear fruit, so that it will be clean and bear more fruit. You have been made clean already by the teaching I have given you. Remain united to me, and I will remain united to you. A branch cannot bear fruit by itself; it can do so only if it remains in the vine. In the same way you cannot bear fruit unless you remain in me.

"I am the vine, and you are the branches. Those who remain in me, and I in them, will bear much fruit; for you can do nothing without me. Those who do not remain in me are thrown out like a branch and dry up; such branches are gathered up and thrown into the fire, where they are burned. If you remain in me and my words remain in you, then you will ask for anything you wish, and you shall have it. My Father's glory is shown by your bearing much fruit; and in this way you become my disciples. I love you just as the Father loves me; remain in my love. If you obey my commands, you

will remain in my love, just as I have obeyed my Father's commands and remain in his love. (John 15:1-10)

A branch represents your church grafted to the shaft of the lampstand with its light. The light feeds and guides us in its path. If we are to tell the Church about this light, then we have to tell them about Christ, because He is the light of the lampstand. We share the word of God with people, but do we share the light with them? What is this light, and what is its purpose in our lives? We share stories about God, but do we ever share His light with people?

• There are six branches extending from the shaft of the lampstand, but who are these branches?

• Who are the people that make up the six branches of the lampstand?

• Is it the faithless, the unbeliever, the anointed, or the uncalled?

• Who are they?

• Jesus has come for all, so who are the "all"? The answer lies within us.

• Who do we call ourselves? Are we the children of God? If we are, then Jesus came for us. We are His mission and strength. Without us, He has no mission or strength, because it is through His sacrifice for us that He draws His strength. It is through us that His mission is accomplished. So, we need to know who we are in Him, for Him to achieve His mission. We are the Church extended from Him, and the people He needs to save.

> *The woman said to him, "I know that the Messiah will come, and when he comes, <u>he will tell us everything.</u>" Jesus answered, "I am he, I who am talking with you"* (Emphasis added, John 4:25-26).

The Messiah knows everything in the law, because He is the law. As the Samaritan woman proclaimed to the people of her town, she has found a man who told her everything that she had ever done and everything that she needed to know.

> *Then the woman left her water jar, went back to the town, and said to the people there, <u>"Come and see the man who told me everything I have ever done. Could he be the Messiah?</u>"* (John 4:28-29).

> <u>*In past times human beings were not told this secret,*</u> *but God has revealed it now by the Spirit to his holy apostles and prophets. The secret is that by means of the gospel the Gentiles have a part with the Jews in God's blessings; they are members of the same body and share in the promise that God made through Christ Jesus* (Emphasis added, Ephesians 3:5-6).

Sacrificing Himself for us was a great accomplishment, but redeeming us from the hands of the enemy is the greatest fulfillment of all. He grafted us to Himself with all our faults, thereby saving us. These branches stand for the individual churches in the Lord, who understands and accepts the work of Christ made on the cross. The Church is a stand and no matter what you do, it will still be a stand. Nothing will change it. There is a difference between the Church of today and the Faithful Church (*a gathering of people with faith*) as described in Revelation 3:7-13.

- What are you building? Are you building a Faithful Church for the Lord?
- What's really the difference between the branches and the Faithful Church?

The branches and the Faithful Church (shaft) as the word says are joined in unison as a single unit. The branches form unison with the shaft by a bud. Christ died for our sins and through His death, we are saved. So, although we sinned against God, He has pardoned us through the blood of Jesus Christ if you believe in Him. He becomes the sacrificial lamb. If you believe in Him, you will be like a tree planted by the rivers of water (Psalms 1:3). If you live your life according to the way the world lives it, then He will cut that branch off from Him. You will live in the hell of fire (*this world*).

For Christ himself has brought us peace by making Jews and Gentiles one people. With his own body he broke down the wall that separated them and kept them enemies. He abolished the Jewish Law with its commandments and rules, in order to create out of the two races one new people in union with himself, in this way making peace. By his death on the cross Christ destroyed their enmity; by means of the cross he united both races into one body and brought them back to God. So Christ came and preached the Good News of peace to all—to you Gentiles, who were far away from God, and to the Jews, who were near to him. It is through Christ that all of us, Jews and Gentiles, are able to come in the one Spirit into the presence of the Father (Ephesians 2:14-18).

The branches are to bring peace to the world, but are we? The branches come with buds and petals. They have to be productive. The buds are attached to critical points where they develop petals. The petals are uniquely designed in shape and color to attract pollinators and surround the productive parts of the flower. We are the buds to keep the branch in place and secured. We are to bring the Church to its place on the lampstand. The light is within us. You and I have been positioned in a place where we will bring the oneness to the Church. We are to unite the Church as one through His word.

The six branches proceed out from the shaft for a reason. However, without the six branches, our salvation would have been questionable. The branches stand for the grace of our Lord Jesus Christ on us, without which we would have been lost. That is what the Word is saying to the Church. We should worship the Lord our God with all our heart and strength. Jesus Christ is our Savior.

The size of the lampstand indicates the worship of God in us. It houses seven lamps and the Faithful Church in the middle of it. The decorative flowers are there, indicating our involvement in bringing this vision to pass—lightening up the world with His word.

The Spirit in the Holy of Holies is that of the resurrected Christ in whom we believe. The lampstand brings illumination to the Holy Place; it gives that realm its light of understanding. It brings us the light that guides our path as we walk through the Holy Place. It brightens every corner of the room—the illumination of God's word.

The Word of God Brings Illumination!

Why Grafting?

Grafting brings perfection to the Church. To be grafted, the Church needs to put some structures in place to meet the standards of grafting. You do not just get grafted to the Faithful Church, it requires self-sacrifice to be successfully grafted into it.

Grafting is a principle to be followed and this principle is in the word of the LORD.

Grafting is for the lost and the blind. The need to be grafted to Christ is something that needs to be done in order to meet the entry requirement for the Holy of Holies. You need to share in the Lord's suffering and righteousness to be able to approach God's mercy seat. The lampstand stands for equal standings.

God gave the Church the vision of Christ for the purpose of grafting into Christ by the sacrifice that He made on the cross. It is a process that was put in place before the creation of this world. God had already put this lampstand in place for our transgressions. He foretold the story by preparing the lampstand before its time. We are in the season of making His will come to pass. Whatever He said in the past (Old Testament scriptures) is about to happen in the present. We are living the present, and His will is being established. The cross is to be carried, but by whom?

Jesus Christ is the cross on Calvary and we join Him on the cross by grafting. We were grafted to the cross for our salvation. Grafting is all about Christ's sacrifice on the cross and our acceptance of His work on it. We share in His righteousness through grafting which makes us one with Him. The grafted Church becomes spiritually fruitful. Jesus is our bridge to God—our Creator. It is through Christ that our salvation will come, therefore grafting us into Him. We come to the cross of Jesus for the salvation of our souls, and He in turn, leads us to our faith. Grafting is for our faith in God and resurrection is our journey in God. So, we lean on

God for our salvation and He brings us out of our misery. This is what God calls "salvation"—the grafting of the six branches to the shaft of the lampstand. This is salvation—God bringing and making us one in Him. We share the same idea, principles and love each other—that is oneness in the LORD.

Christianity is about oneness in the Lord, but we have changed the meaning of Christianity to our own version, which is Christ for us all, but each one for himself. That is not love. We do not love with division; we love to unite and that unity lies within God. So, we cannot call ourselves Christians if we do not love each other as Jesus has taught us. We are liars in that sense. Christianity is about love and unity, and not division. We do not discriminate; we are one. No matter what our differences are, we unite. That is Christianity. We are only Christians if we love. We are followers of Christ, and He is love.

- Are we Christians if we do not love?
- Are we Christians if we discriminate?

Discrimination is the weapon of destruction. You cannot love and then discriminate at the same time. You cannot fall in love with someone, and then apart with the person. Love conquers all and shames all the iniquities of life. Discrimination breeds hatred and hatred produces anger, which in turn brings about war. War and peace are not the same. War brings division and peace brings unity. So, do not war among yourselves as division is not good. Do not bring division among yourselves. We are fighting a great war against Evil, and waring each other will not bring fruition. We need to unite to fight the evil of this world.

For us to be who God wants us to be, we must be grafted to the cross of Jesus Christ, to share His loving-kindness in us. The process of grafting six branches into the lampstand is the instruction given by God in the construction of the lampstand. With the hammering of the pure gold metal, the six branches were formed in unison with the lampstand.

Make seven lamps for the lampstand and set them up so that they shine toward the front (Exodus 25:37).

Types of Grafting Techniques

There are different kinds of grafting and each defines a particular church. Each church has a different problem(s) and the technique for grafting also changes based on their fault or differences.

All the different techniques yield oneness. Although all the branches extend from the shaft of the lampstand, they all are not the same. The churches bring restoration to themselves by living by the will of God.

As the Church grafts in to the shaft of the lampstand, the people of the Church buds to the grafted Church. The grafted Church is to feed the buds through the strength gained from the lampstand. The grafted Church feeds the people of the Church through budding. This is the purpose of the Church—seeking the face of God every day to feed His people. In order to do so, it has to be grafted to the lampstand.

The Church cannot be outside of the will of God to receive His light. It needs to proceed out of the shaft to receive His light and create oneness. At certain points on the extended branch, the bud put in place represents the union of the Church with its people. The Church becomes one with the Cross. As we bud to our respective churches, it feeds, grows, and brings us into oneness with Christ.

We have grafting and budding of the Church. The budding feeds us with the word of God, and grafting brings us into oneness with the Lord. At the moment, we are far away from the cross and His oneness. But the word of God will come to us, and when it reaches us, we shall be one with Him. The word will hammer us into shape with the shaft of the lampstand. The construction of oneness is through Christ, and our understanding of the lampstand is also through Him.

Tools used in grafting and budding.
- Pruning shears
- Budding knife
- Grafting knife
- Cleft-grafting chisel
- Wax
- Tying materials

Most of the tools used in grafting are used in cutting through, sawing the rootstock and the scion at a specific angle, and joining the two parts together with a grafting clip.

Jesus and the Grafter

God spoke about the branches being extended from the sides of the lampstand. He is talking about the Church and its growth. We cannot talk about grafting and branches without mentioning and visiting the Samaritan woman at Jacob's well in the Gospel of John chapter 4. All she needed was acceptance and affirmation from the Lord through her faith.

The Pharisees heard that Jesus was winning and baptizing more disciples than John. (Actually, Jesus himself did not baptize anyone; only his disciples did.) So when Jesus heard what was being said, he left Judea and went back to Galilee; on his way there he had to go through Samaria. In Samaria he came to a town named Sychar, which was not far from the field that Jacob had given to his son Joseph. Jacob's well was there, and Jesus, tired out by the trip, sat down by the well. It was about noon.

A Samaritan woman came to draw some water, and Jesus said to her, "Give me a drink of water." (His disciples had gone into town to buy food.)

The woman answered, "You are a Jew, and I am a Samaritan—so how can you ask me for a drink?" (Jews will not use the same cups and bowls that Samaritans use.)

Jesus answered, "If you only knew what God gives and who it is that is asking you for a drink, you would ask him, and he would give you life-giving water."

"Sir," the woman said, "you don't have a bucket, and the well is deep. Where would you get that life-giving water? It was our ancestor Jacob who gave us this well; he and his children and his flocks all drank from it. You don't claim to be greater than Jacob, do you?"

Jesus answered, "Those who drink this water will get thirsty again, but those who drink the water that I will give them will never be thirsty again. The water that I will give them will become in them a spring which will provide them with life-giving water and give them eternal life."

"Sir," the woman said, "give me that water! Then I will never be thirsty again, nor will I have to come here to draw water."

"Go and call your husband," Jesus told her, "and come back."

"I don't have a husband," she answered.

Jesus replied, "You are right when you say you don't have a husband. You have been married to five men, and the man you live with now is not really your husband. You have told me the truth."

"I see you are a prophet, sir," the woman said. "My Samaritan ancestors worshiped God on this mountain, but you Jews say that Jerusalem is the place where we should worship God."

Jesus said to her, "Believe me, woman, the time will come when people will not worship the Father either on this mountain or in Jerusalem. You Samaritans do not really know whom you worship; but we Jews know whom we worship, because it is from the Jews that salvation comes. But the time is coming and is already here, when by the power of God's Spirit people will worship the Father as he really is, offering him the true worship that he wants. God is Spirit, and only by the power of his Spirit can people worship him as he really is."

The woman said to him, "I know that the Messiah will come, and when he comes, he will tell us everything."

Jesus answered, "I am he, I who am talking with you."

At that moment Jesus' disciples returned, and they were greatly surprised to find him talking with a woman. But none of them said to her, "What do you want?" or asked him, "Why are you talking with her?"

Then the woman left her water jar, went back to the town, and said to the people there, "Come and see the man who told me everything I have ever done. Could he be the Messiah?" So they left the town and went to Jesus. In the meantime the disciples were begging Jesus, "Teacher, have something to eat!"

But he answered, "I have food to eat that you know nothing about."

So the disciples started asking among themselves, "Could somebody have brought him food?"

"My food," Jesus said to them, "is to obey the will of the one who sent me and to finish the work he gave me to do. You have a saying, 'Four more months and then the harvest.' But I tell you, take a good look at the fields; the crops are now ripe and ready to be harvested! The one who reaps the harvest is being paid and gathers the crops for eternal life; so the one who plants and the one who reaps will be glad together. For the saying is true, 'Someone plants, someone else reaps.' I have sent you to reap a harvest in a field where you did not work; others worked there, and you profit from their work."

Many of the Samaritans in that town believed in Jesus because the woman had said, "He told me everything I have ever done." So when the Samaritans came to him, they begged him to stay with them, and Jesus stayed there two days.

Many more believed because of his message, and they told the woman, "We believe now, not because of what you said, but because we ourselves have heard him, and we know that he really is the Savior of the world." (John 4:1-42)

Jesus stopped by Jacob's well because He was tired from His journey, traveling from Judea back to Galilee through Samaria. Still, according to the Jewish laws, He is not meant to associate Himself with a Samaritan, but He has relations with Jacob's well. It is part of Him. He is not intended to be seen anywhere in Samaria or share anything with a Samaritan. Still, He went through Samaria against the laws for the will of God to established—Union.

At the well, a Samaritan woman met Jesus as she came to draw water. At the well, Jesus spoke with her. They shared intimate secrets, and there, the Lord saved her by offering her His companionship. He related to her in ways that no one understood, and He shared His will with her by providing her the eternal life in Him. All she thirsts for (acceptance and affirmation), Jesus accepted and affirmed her through her faith.

He shared His will with her through faith and ushered her into His will—that is grafting. Although she is not with Him, He still accepted her as she was and grafted her in Him. This is the simple symposium of who Christ is—*the Savior.* Jesus came to bring down those invisible and visible barriers and break down deception.

The above text reveals Jesus giving a revelation of what God gives to His children and His true nature to the Samaritan woman. Jesus asked the Samaritan woman to quench His thirst, and He will, in turn, quench hers with His life-giving water.

- Why did Jesus present Himself as life-giving water to the Samaritan woman?
- Why the need for water to quench her thirst?

They were on common ground and the common ground is the well of Jacob. Because she came to the well to draw water, so He associated Himself with her as the life-giving water.

He is the life-giving water to the Samaritans. He quenches their thirst in the time of need. He is the One to bring them out of the need that they have, rising above their unacceptance. Jesus becomes their rootstock to which they will be grafted; He will fill them up and make them acceptable. The Samaritans became grafted to Jesus for acceptance. His life-giving water nourishes them and gives them eternal life. Life-giving water is who Jesus is to the unaccepted and those that are considered "unclean."

Comparing verses 5 & 12, Jesus came from the House of Jacob through the line of David. In verse 12, the Samaritan woman claims that Jacob, their ancestor, his children, and his flock, all drank from this well.

- What is the difference between the two, is it the cups and bowls?

He is a Jew, and she is a Samaritan, but the Jews do not drink from the same cups and bowls as the Samaritans. The difference is the sharing of the same cup and bowl, and their ancestor, Jacob, his children, and flocks, all drank from this well.

- Who is this Samaritan woman at the well?

She is the laws of the land, holding them bondage.

For the Church to become grafted to the cross on Calvary, our work of revival needs doing in order not to fail the process. The Church is in its dying need to fulfill the will of God. Destiny has been written, but it is in the hands of the Beholder.

Try not to mess up your destiny for the sake of the world. Bring your destiny in line with the will of God.

The old and the new meet at the well—Jesus being the New Covenant that heals the soul and also the Church to come. He is the life-giving Water that heals the soul of man and not the man-made well. This explains the grafting of the Old Church to the New Church.

In Him is the life-giving water and those who drink the water He gives will never thirst again. The water will become in them a spring which will provide them with life-giving water and life eternal. He is the Faithful Church revealed to John in Revelation 1.

Vv. 7-15 - This is the conversation that went on between Jesus and the Samaritan woman, but Jesus did not reveal Himself to her until she saw the miracle He could do.

- You are asking me for water, but then you claim to be a provider of life-giving water?

- Where is your bucket to draw the water as the well is deep?

- Where would you find this life-giving water?

These are the two accomplishments she gave Jesus. She also made two astonishing statements to Jesus: *you are a provider of life-giving water, but where is your bucket as the well is deep and you do not claim to be greater than Jacob, do you?* However, Jesus answered her by giving her the story of her ancestors—this is my bucket and you are at my well. The well is deep but it is my story. If only you knew who it is asking you for a drink of water and what He gives.

The well is Jesus' story and He elaborated the story to the woman. This is the well of His forefather. He left this well here for our purpose—for a day such as this. He dug the well for us to meet each other today, whether Jew or Samaritan.

Before Jesus met the Samaritan woman by Jacob's well on His way from Judea back to Galilee, He had a dialogue with a Jewish leader called Nicodemus in the previous chapter (John 4:1-21) about the principle of eternal life in Christ Jesus. The Jewish leader belonged to a party of the Pharisees. And as Jesus met the Samaritan woman by the well, He introduced the love of God to her as the principle of eternal life in Christ Jesus.

Jesus spoke about the love of God in Him and showed the woman who the love of God is. See how He introduced to each of them the love of God and the discipline behind it. He did not show them the same magnitude as He showed everyone. He gave them the principle and ask them to define it for themselves; one is a teacher and the other is just a laywoman who knew nothing about Him. He gave them the principle to digest and see the result of it.

Previously, He had spoken to Nicodemus about eternal life in John 3:1-21, where He elaborated on the meaning of eternal life. He says in verse 3 that no one can see the Kingdom of God without being born again. That was the beginning of His argument. The talk about the Kingdom of God, that all are waiting and working hard for, cannot be seen without being born again by water and the Spirit. The physical manifestation of oneself is different from the Spiritual manifestation. So, even though we are born of the flesh by our human parents, we need to be spiritually reborn through faith in Christ. And anyone reborn of the Spirit worships the Father in Spirit and in truth.

The great teacher in Israel did not know how to be born again by the Spirit, as people are already grown men. The Lord said to Him, you do things in the physical—repetitive rituals in the name of the Kingdom of God, but unless a man is born of the Spirit, he cannot see the Kingdom of God. Yes, you know who you worship, but the Kingdom of God will not come from your physical connections or rituals with God, but from your heart, which needs circumcision. Accept Jesus Christ as your Savior, believe in Him and have eternal life (John 3:16). He is the eternal life.

Although, you are a great nation, you lack the presence of God through His Son, Jesus Christ. He is eternal life and in Him is the spring of water that never dries. He is the river of life. So, Jesus told the Samaritan woman in John 4:21-24 that a time will come when people will not worship the Father either on this mountain as Samaritans do or in Jerusalem like the Jews. Why? Because God is Spirit, and it is only by the power of His Spirit can all offer Him <u>the true worship</u> He desires.

To the Samaritans – You worship God on this mountain, but you do not REALLY know whom you worship. You need to <u>drink water from the well of Jesus</u>. This water will become a spring in you which will provide you with life-giving water and give you eternal life. Those who drink from it will never cry for thirst again.

Jesus answered, "If you only knew what God gives and who it is that is asking you for a drink, you would ask him, and he would give you life-giving water" (John 4:10).

Jesus answered, "Those who drink this water will get thirsty again, but those who drink the water that I will give them will never be thirsty again. The water that I will give them will become in them a spring which will provide them with life-giving water and give them eternal life" (John 4:13-14).

And to the Jews – you know whom you worship, because it is from the Jews that salvation comes. But all need to <u>be born of water and Spirit</u> to receive eternal life.

> *As Moses lifted up the bronze snake on a pole in the desert, in the same way the Son of Man must be lifted up, so that everyone who believes in him may have eternal life. For God loved the world so much that he gave his only Son, so that everyone who believes in him may not die but have eternal life. For God did not send his Son into the world to be its judge, but to be its savior.* (John 3:14-17).

Jesus is here today at the well to provide you with His life-giving water and eternal life, but He is first asking you to give Him a drink of water. Put your trust in Him first.

- Jesus Christ is the rootstock (John 4:25-26) and also the root system—the Rock foundation.
- The Samaritan woman being the scion (John 4:28-29) and becoming the shooting system.

The word of God becomes the rootstock on which they will be grafted to and God is the grafter. He grafts us to the Faithful Church; Jesus Christ, the giver of eternal life and life-giving water.

The branches share the same life-giving water, although they are physically not the same and mentally different. The

Samaritan woman and the many who believed in the message of Jesus were grafted to Jesus.

She is classified as an outcast and need not be near Jesus, but Jesus accepted her by stopping by the well where she draws her water. He does not have to be there but He is. He did not have to share His well with her, but He did. This is the love of God. When things seem different and incompatible, He breaks the rules and makes it feasible. He does not share His love because He needs to, but He does so because He is love and love resides in Him. This is the mystery of the well—to give love to the unlovable. Drink from my well, Jesus said to the Samaritan woman who did not deserve to drink from Him. But Jesus offered His help first. Jesus offered to drink from the woman, until the woman refused to offer Him water as she was not worthy to be in His presence as being judged unclean.

Christ came for all—both clean and unclean [as Noah was instructed to carry into the Ark seven pairs of each kind of ritually clean but one pair of each kind of unclean animal (Genesis 7:1-3)]. Likewise, the word of God covers both clean and the unclean. It is salvation. It has to be rooted in us. Jesus knew who she was and still offered her His life-giving water. That is the story of the creation of the *Uni-verse*. Us being the dictator of our soul and Him being the rescuer. This is about salvation and the cross.

- We lean against the cross for salvation but will our souls be healed?

- Salvation is a long path, but will our souls be healed from the past?

He knew who we were and still came to us. He knew our sins and still birth to us His Son. He knew who we were, and still allowed His Son to be born to us and give us salvation. We became grafted to the Lord Jesus Christ for our salvation and prosperity. Blessed be the Lord Jesus Christ! God grafted us into the Lord Jesus Christ—the perfection.

The Samaritan woman was the one in need and Christ was the one to provide her the peace she has been longing for. He is the resolution to her problem. She has been married to five men and even the man she was living with at the time of their meeting was not really her husband. She had no stability in her life, but still comes to Jacob's well to draw water.

- *Does that sound like you? Always in the presence of God, but nothing works for you. Do you have a need that needs meeting by Jesus?*

The Samaritan woman has a need and Jesus met this need at the well. He saved her and brought her to fruition. He sanctified her and made her whole—that is the spiritual side of the story—making the impossible possible.

With all our sins, Jesus came to save us. He did not walk away from us, but walked with us to bring us to fruition. He isolated our problem and saw us as we are, the children of the Most High God, the forbidden generation out of rest. He looked up to us and did not ignore or look down on us. He resurrected us from our graves. He brought peace to us and established us in God's Kingdom. Although we were failing, He did not ignore us. He brought us love. Jesus stayed by the will of God.

V. 40 Jesus stayed with the Samaritans for another two days. The people believed in Him and His work and everything He stood for and He became their Savior.

Vv. 37-38 says for the saying is true: "Someone plants, someone else reaps." God has sent you to reap a harvest in a field where you did not work; others worked there, and you profit from their work.

God grafted the Samaritans to Jesus Christ using the woman as a bud holding their cut surfaces together to heal.

Vv. 41 says many more believed because of His message. They grew into the shoot system of the Church.

Sometimes, things do not always happen the way we want them, but they are all the good. Because as the earth remains, seedtime and harvest shall remain. We can always make up for the time but when we live according to our will, then the consequences of our will become a problem. We live for God and He for us. Let us live according to His will. The Lord is with us and will always be.

This is what God is saying to the world: *He is grafting us into His Church.* None will be left out, but coming to the cross of Jesus Christ is the only way to the Church. God demands His people to worship Him in truth and in spirit. He has called upon His children to live a life of self-sacrifice (meaning: *the sacrifice of one's own desires, interest, etc, for the sake of duty or for the well-being of others*).

A Call for Repentance

The messages to the seven churches were a call for repentance. It identified the strength and weaknesses of each church and commended them to change their ways. It is a wake-up call to the churches to gird up their loins and saddle their horses for the coming of Christ.

God has ordained us to be His children, but some of us have broken off from His tree. They have set up their own rules and living them. He is calling us to His throne room. We should wear our clothes of righteousness to show how far we have deviated from the Church. God is calling everyone to Himself. Let those who have ears hear His servant's call. Let us hear the voice of the One in the wilderness calling for repentance for the end is near.

As the time drew near when Jesus would be taken up to heaven, he made up his mind and set out on his way to Jerusalem. He sent messengers ahead of him, who went into a village in Samaria to get everything ready for him. But the people there would not receive him, because it was clear that he was on his way to Jerusalem. When the disciples James and John saw this, they said, "Lord, do you want us to call fire down from heaven to destroy them?" Jesus turned and rebuked them. Then Jesus and his disciples went on to another village (Luke 9:52-56).

The LORD is calling the Church to Himself for salvation. The end of this world is near! The Lord is calling His faithful servant to Himself. Repentance is needed in order to be grafted to the Faithful Church, like John the Baptist as a voice in the wilderness calls for repentance. The time for repentance is now and <u>not</u> tomorrow. Tomorrow has its own worries. It is now or never! Repent, Church, for the LORD is calling!

Repentance is a problem in the Church. The LORD is calling us to repentance before the time of His coming. Grafting us to the cross of Jesus brings repentance, because we look up to Him for salvation. We are to follow His footsteps and enter His grace to fulfill the will of God—accomplishment. We need to be grafted to Christ to achieve what our purpose is in Him.

To do so, we have to go through the cutting, sawing, pruning, and planting. This is the process we have to go through before the planting. We cannot be ourselves in achieving what God wants us to achieve. We have to go through lamentation to come out good. We need to be good for the Lord. Christ is for us all—the whole community. It is now up to us how we value and see Him.

The Church is in a hurry to close service, but it is in a world where salvation is!

- Why is the Church in a hurry to close service when all she needs is this world lacking salvation?

We have so much work to do than we think. Jesus, in John 4:35, said to His disciples to take a good look at the fields; the crops are now ripe and ready to be harvested. Open your eyes to this world and see its readiness to be saved by Christ, but all that the Church can see is the troubles of this world and its divisions.

It might not be how you presume it to be, but the world is ready for God's salvation. It is in a position where salvation is prepared to come to it, but the Church is in a hurry to close its service. It is not fulfilling the Commission the Lord gave it in Matthew 28:16-20. It is running away from the harvest because the Commission involves commitment, self-sacrifice, long-suffering, pain, love, and dedication. You cannot go through life without pain. The Church has to go through some acclaimed prohibited lands—it has to reach out to those it does not share the same beliefs with. It has to do what is not the norm. It is easier for the Church to say they believe in God instead of fulfilling His will. And it is easier to say we are followers of Jesus Christ than to share in His sufferings.

The Church Is In A Hurry To Close...

The Church is failing in a world that needs it to be prominent in its decision-making. This cannot be said, but it is failing the world of its moral system. It has to stand up to its high morals in raising champions for the Lord. The Church needs to embrace the word of God and show the world where she stands. In these last days, if the Church refuses to define what she stands for, the world will dictate to the Church what her beliefs should be. The Church is on her last legs and needs revival, if not, the world will take over the Church and give her definitions.

When God spoke about the six branches extending from the sides of the lampstand in Exodus 25:31-40, He was talking about the growth of the Church by grafting. The instructions for the construction of the lampstand were all about God's oneness of the Church. This process is to bring or graft these churches into the Faithful Church. The Faithful Church is Jesus Christ.

You cannot talk about the Church, grafting, and branches without mentioning or visiting the Samaritan woman at Jacob's well in the Gospel of John chapter 4:1-42.

The seven golden lampstands represent the seven churches in the equal division. God shares among them the same anointing and judgment. Jesus is the lampstand in the Holy Place that provides illumination. He is the light of the lampstand and in the Holy Place.

Jesus said to her, "Believe me, woman, the time will come when people will not worship the Father either on this mountain or in Jerusalem. You Samaritans do not really know whom you worship; but we Jews know whom we

worship, because it is from the Jews that salvation comes. But the time is coming and is already here, when by the power of God's Spirit people will worship the Father as he really is, offering him the true worship that he wants. God is Spirit, and only by the power of his Spirit can people worship him as he really is"
(John 4:21-24).

Chapter Five

Deposits of His Faith

The hammering brings out the faith we possess via the message received through the servants of Jesus. Therefore, the messages go out to the churches in preparation for harvest. The message is the important instrument in the hammering of pure gold. The hammering of your faith by the message brings about your salvation. It also brings out the strength in you. Without the messages to the seven churches, salvation becomes elusive—there is no purpose of the pure gold. God gave the instrument for the hammering. The message was used for the hammering. The hammer was the message.

The Authentic Word

God deposits His faith with the churches through communication. He ministers to the crowd with His Word as the Word is with us in the Church. He lectures us on His Word through His servants. He is now ministering to us through His Word, which was given to us before the foundation of the world. His Word will stand until the Lord comes. His Word will remain the same.

God has given us His Word to preach and teach. May we continue to do so until He comes for the Church? Praise be to our Lord Jesus Christ! Share the Word of faith with everyone! Be God's champion in upholding His faith.

I am about to share a message that God, in His infinite Self, has given me to share with the churches. As I received this message, I am sharing it with you.

This is the word from the Most High God. Thus says the Lord:

I AM THE LORD YOUR GOD WHO COMETH NOT BUT AMONG HIS PEOPLE. I HAVE COME IN ORDER TO BRING YOU TOGETHER IN ACCORDANCE WITH MY WILL—THE RULE OF ONENESS IN THE LORD. I STAND AMONG YOU, CHURCHES, AS THE GOD OF YOUR SUPPLIES. I SUPPLY YOU OF ALL YOUR NEEDS ACCORDING TO MY RICHES IN HEAVEN. I HAVE COME TO ANNOUNCE TO YOU OF MY COMING (RE-

DEMPTION), AND ON THAT DAY, LITTLE WILL BE KNOWN TO YOU. I WILL BE ANNOUNCING MY COMING THROUGH MY SON, AND I WILL MAKE MY WILL BE KNOWN TO HIM.

LITTLE DID THEY KNOW THAT I CREATED A CREATURE AMONG YOU WHO WILL AN-NOUNCE MY COMING. THAT'S WHY I SAID, "THE DAY OF THE COMING OF MY SON IS NOT IN HIS HANDS, BUT IN MY HANDS, THE CREATOR. HE HAS NO IDEA WHEN, BUT IT WOULD BE ANNOUNCED IN THE CHURCHES TO COME. I HAVE SET A PLACE FOR YOU, AND I HAVE SET MY PLANS FOR YOU. THE COMING OF THE LORD WILL BE LIKE A FLASH. HE IS HERE ONE MINUTE AND NEXT HE IS GONE.

I HAVE CREATED MY WAYS AMONG YOU TO SET UP A FAITHFUL CHURCH. WITH THAT FAITHFUL CHURCH, I WILL ESTABLISH MY COVENANT WITH HER. SO I AM COMING TO YOU TO ESTABLISH THAT FAITH-RIDDEN CHURCH, AND WITH FAITH, ALL THINGS ARE POSSIBLE.

I HAVE MANAGED TO PUT THINGS TO-GETHER IN YOUR CHURCH, AND I HAVE SENT MY MESSENGER WITH YOUR MESSAGE, BUT <u>WOE</u> UNTO ANYONE WHO REFUSES TO LISTEN TO MY SON! I WILL SET THEM APART

(SEGREGATE THEM) AND POUR MY OIL OF CONDEMNATION ON THEM BECAUSE I AM COMING IN STRONG WITH MY WHIP IN MY HAND AND MY SCROLL. I WILL WHIP ANYONE WHO DISOBEYS ME, AND I WILL RESTORE MY PROMISE TO ANYONE WHO LISTENS TO MY VOICE. THE LORD IS COMING AND QUICKLY AS WELL.

I WISH ALL WILL ADHERE TO MY MESSAGE AND MAKE A WAY TO MY RESURRECTION TABLE, BUT THE ENEMY IS AT LARGE AND IS CAUSING HAVOC AMONG YOU. <u>WOE</u> UNTO HIM THAT BELIEVES IN THE ENEMY! HE SHALL BE LIKE THE FRUIT EATEN BY THE WOMAN; IT SHALL HURT HIM FOREVER. BUT IF YOU ARE FAITHFUL TO MY WORD, THEN I WILL GIVE YOU THE KEYS OF LIFE TO MY MANSION, WHERE YOU WILL RESIDE FOR THE KINGDOM TO COME AND THIS KINGDOM TO PASS.

I HAVE ESTABLISHED MY RULES, AND MY RULES STAND. <u>WOE</u> UNTO ANYONE WHO TRIES TO CHANGE IT! IT SHOULD BE LIKE THE DAYS OF NOAH; HE SHALL DIE IN THE STORM OF THE LORD. I AM CONVEYING THIS MESSAGE THROUGH YOU TO PROCLAIM MY DAY OF JUDGMENT WHEN I, THE LORD, WILL COME TO JUDGE THE WORLD OF ITS

SIN. I WILL CLEAR YOU OFF YOUR SIN AND MOVE YOU INTO MY WORLD AND RESTORE TO YOU MY PROMISE OF GREAT PEACE ON EARTH. MY CHILDREN WILL LIVE FOREVER AND EVER.

LET THIS BE A MESSAGE TO YOU, THAT I, THE LORD, AM A JEALOUS GOD WHO WOULD NOT ENTERTAIN ANY IDOL WORSHIPPING IN MY CHURCH. SO I HAVE A RULE THAT ANYONE WHO LOVES ME SHOULD LOVE ME IN THEIR HEART, MIND, AND SOUL. IN THAT CASE, THEY WILL NOT FORGET ME AND LET ANY IDOL BE THEIR GOD. REPUTATION IS WHY YOU ARE GOING AND DESTINATION IS WHERE YOU WILL GO, BUT WILL BE REJECTED FOR YOUR WORD.

I AM TELLING YOU; I AM A JEALOUS GOD AND WILL NOT TAKE SUCH AS A JOKE. I AM COMING AND WILL NOT DELAY FOR ANY REASON.

THE LORD IS MY SHEPHERD; I SHALL NOT WANT…PSALMS 23.

THE BREAD OF LIFE IS JESUS, MY SON, WHO CAME TO BE WITH YOU AND IS WITH YOU AND WILL BE WITH YOU. AMEN! PRAISE BE TO GOD! HALLELUJAH!!

This is the word of God to the Church. He has given us His Word on the Church, and it shall stand in Jesus' name. The serpent shall spend all its days crawling on its belly, and will have to eat dust as long as it lives. This is a warning to the Church that disobeys God.

> *Then the* LORD *God said to the snake, "You will be punished for this; you alone of all the animals must bear this curse: <u>From now on you will crawl on your belly, and you will have to eat dust as long as you live.</u> I will make you and the woman hate each other; her offspring and yours will always be enemies. Her offspring will crush your head, and you will bite her offspring's heel."* (Genesis 3:14-15)

The Letters

In the Book of Revelation chapters 2 through 3, we see the letters sent to the seven churches from Christ through His servant, John, about the churches and their standing with God. The letters to the churches indicate where they stand in the Word of God. The letters briefly tell you who you are when it comes to the things of God. The letters simplify in context what we are doing to stop God's blessings on our life. We perhaps anticipated changing the laws of God in the Church to suit us, but the law is the law. It cannot be changed neither can it be altered in any way because God is the Law. God is God, and nothing you do can change Him.

He is an omnipotent God about whom Matthew 5:18 says:

Remember that as long as heaven and earth last, not the least point nor the smallest detail of the Law will be done away with, not until the end of all things (Matthew 5:18).

Heaven and earth will pass away, but my words will never pass away (Matthew 24:35).

The letters that went out were very strong. God's message to the churches approaches us in our time of need. When all is lost and nothing can be found, then the Lord shows up to make a difference. Life is not about one person but everyone. The Word of God is about everybody—not about one person alone!

- How can people see themselves as being superior to other human beings simply because of their race?
- Where did we learn that the Most High God is a respecter of persons—let alone a particular race?

The Lord came for us **all**; therefore, there is no difference in His love for any particular generation or race.

- What part of the Bible tells us that the Lord is partial in His judgment and love toward us?

He gives us equal grace.

- He gave up His life to be able to rescue us from the pit of hell, so why do we classify ourselves as being more important than others?

- Take a look at your watch, does it tell you the time of the day?

So does the love of God cover everywhere and everyone; no human race is superior to another.

In the eyes of God, we are ALL His children and who are we to discriminate against what God has created? The law of the land says, *"You shall not take the name of the* LORD *your God in vain"* (Exodus 20:7; ESV). Discriminating among God's creation is calling God's name in vain and insulting His intelligence in creating the human race. Look at the world and see what is happening. Calling upon God for His blessings is a shame because we do not deserve them. Unfortunately, we creatures of displeasure do not appreciate what God has given us, and we create our own creations in the name of God.

Let us heed the voice of God; if not, we will ALL end up in the fire of the furnace, and this time, the fourth person who looks like an angel (Jesus Christ) who got in the blazing furnace with Shadrach, Meshach, and Abednego will not be in the furnace with us. As we are pushed into the ends of the world, it is only our faith in Him that will save us.

We must listen to the voice of God and change our ways as the days are getting shorter and nearer. A piece of advice is to be devoted to the Lord because, without His strength, we will not be able to withstand the pressures of the world coming. We need His devotion and His love to survive in this world. We must teach our children how to pray in the words of the Father because they will need prayer power in times of strife. They will need to search for the Father in their hearts as the time approaches.

Difficult times are approaching in this world; the fine vineyards we once knew will be overgrown with thorns, bushes, and briers (Isaiah 7:23-25). Take a fresh note of God's Word every day and make it your daily living bread to sustain you. The evil days are getting closer, and the Lord is in His sanctuary, waiting for you. The generous people will live longer regardless of their pain, but the lovers of the world will sustain injuries because of their beliefs.

The letters to the churches represent those who think all is well with them—not knowing they lack much as they progress through this life. Cultures and traditions are good, but they are long past. Those in deep distress need a revival in their life as the Lord approaches them.

The ancient days are gone and are no more. We are behind with the things of God because our culture has made it so. The Lord came to us as a child born to the young woman, and He is yet to be received as the Son. His message has been preached, and yet the world has not seen or received Him. You have much but cannot seem to make good use of it. You are lost with time. You have canopied yourself in a great wall and need a revival to bring you out. God has a plan laid down for you to come out of your canopy.

You need to know who Jesus is. He is your Messiah (*the Savior*) who is to come. He has come to you, but you could not recognize Him in His humble state (*without the royal robes*) of coming as a lamb. You thought of Him as someone else. He is the King of all kings and the Lord of all lords.

- Are we preaching about God's word or the word of the world?

Because difficult times are approaching and the Church needs the unwavering faith, where they will stay in their faith, and not bow to any other god. We need that faith to war the world. There will be no miracle chasing.

The churches mentioned in the letter are those in need of help from God to survive the great monster. The letter says we are good in our ways, but lack God's wisdom and fear. The Lord will put His wisdom and fear in us in order to sustain us till the end of the struggle when He comes. He will make His will known to us, and we shall abide with it till the end of time when He comes to rescue His faithful Church. We are all waiting for Him in our churches.

Blessed are you who will hear His Word, and blessed are you who shall live by His Word and accept it. God will make you a priest in His kingdom of priests to worship and adore Him in His great place in the tabernacle. You shall be the Lord's and His only.

Part Three

The Messengers

"Be ready for whatever comes, dressed for action and with your lamps lit, 36 like servants who are waiting for their master to come back from a wedding feast. When he comes and knocks, they will open the door for him at once.

- Luke 12:35-36

Chapter Six

The Watchful Servants

God revealed the truth of His word to His Son, Jesus Christ, and He made it evident to His disciples, who later passed on the truth to the Church. This is God's miracle and that of the Church. The Word is embedded in the Gospel of Luke. This is how this gospel will be spread and come to man in his desperate need.

The Gospel of Luke speaks about the resurrection of man, about the things to come, and navigates man into the truth of God's word. The book speaks of the *perpetual* ("eternal, permanent, everlasting, unending, ceaseless, unchanging, abiding") will of God. This gospel informs you about who

God is and what He is about. It differentiates between good and bad, and lets man makes his own choice in deciding which path to take. God has negotiated a path for every person, and this path—*the path of righteousness*—should be followed. In the name of Jesus, you should cast out demons, proclaim the glory of the Lord, and defeat principalities.

The Gospel of Luke tells us about the love of God by looking at the principles of love. It gives man an illustration of God's love and the coming of Christ Jehovah in His glory. Luke also tells us how great God's love is and the compassion and mercy He has on us as sinners, giving us a second chance to make things right (Luke 13:6-9). He loves us and forgives us even when we sin. Knowingly sinning separates us from the Father, but when we unknowingly sin, He will have compassion on our getting things right.

Go and sin no more… (John 8:1-11).

***"Be ready for whatever comes, dressed for action** and **with your lamps lit**, like servants who are waiting for their master to come back from a wedding feast. When he comes and knocks, they will open the door for him at once. How happy are those servants whose master finds them awake and ready when he returns! I tell you, he will take off his coat, have them sit down, and will wait on them. How happy they are if he finds them ready, even if he should come at midnight or even later! And you can be* *sure that if the owner of a house knew the time when the thief would come, he would not let the thief break into his house. And you, too, must be ready, because the Son of Man will come at an hour when you are not expecting him"* (Emphasis added, Luke 12:35-40).

Embedded in the Gospel of Luke 12:35-40 are the coming of Christ and the messages that went out to the churches. The twelve chapters of Luke reveal God's thoughts about <u>duplicity</u>, which means the following:

- *Deliberate deceptiveness in behavior or speech*
- *Deception*
- *A fraudulent representation*
- *Deceit—a misleading falsehood*
- *Acting in bad faith*
- *Deception by pretending to entertain one set of intentions while acting under the influence of another*
- *Hypocrisy*
- *Dishonesty*

In verse 35, which says be ready for whatever comes, dressed for action and with your lamps lit, God is urging us to do the following:

1. Be ready for whatever comes
2. Be dressed for action.
3. Keep our lamps lit.

Be ready for whatever comes...

Be ready for whatever comes—either the Master's returning from the wedding feast OR the thief's (i.e., the Enemy) coming to your house unannounced. Whichever way, you have to be prepared.

Why the comparison of the coming of the Son of God to the following four scenarios?

1. Returning from a wedding feast (Matthew 22:2-14; Revelation 19:9)
2. At midnight
3. Even later or just before dawn
4. At an unexpected hour

The uniqueness of this Scripture is, it began with the end statement, "Be ready for whatever comes." God is telling us the end of the Scripture from the beginning before explaining the reason behind what He has said. Within the context of the verse, the following three *paraphrases ("a restatement of a text or passage in another form or other words, often to clarify meaning; expressing the same message in different words")* were used:

1. ...after the wedding feast.
2. ...at midnight
3. ...right before dawn.

Many parables of Jesus are embedded in the context of this Scripture, which addresses messages including the following:

1. The wedding feast

2. God's timing
3. The coming of Christ
4. God's judgment

Verse 35 of the chapter correlates with the following parables:

a. The parable of the wedding feast (Matthew 22:1-14)
b. The parable of the sower (Matthew 13:1-23; Mark 4:1-20, and Luke 8:4-15)
c. The parable of the talent (Matthew 25:14-30)
d. The parable of the gold coin (Luke 19:11-27)
e. The parable of the virgins (Matthew 25:1-13)

"Be ready for whatever comes" talks about:

- The coming of the Master—both His second and third coming
- If He should come in the middle of the night
- Or even later or right before dawn

You should be ready at all times for the presence of God with your loins girded up. According to the Book of Revelation, there is a second (*Revelation 19:1-21*) and a third coming of the Lord. One would be to establish the kingdom of God and the other to take away the kingdom.

You have to be prepared to meet the Lord in any of His comings, and He will establish you in His kingdom. Since man does not know the time (the hour) nor the day (the instance) of His coming, so he must be prepared. He must be in the field cultivating for harvest.

For a time such as this, He will call. Woe to whoever is not fully prepared for His coming. He shall deal with you accordingly. This is the Word of God. God is precise about His timing, and He will never let a moment, a minute, or an hour go past that set time.

How Do You Get Ready with the Word of God?

You get ready by creating a space in your heart to accommodate God's Word and make the Word available to His people. Consider the following parables:

a) The parable of the sower
b) The parable of the talent
c) The parable of the gold coin
d) The parable of the virgins

You can get ready by being in the field dealing with God's work in any of the following ways:

- By proclaiming the Word of God
- Making God known to everyone
- Growing God's kingdom through soul-winning
- Doing kingdom work (healing the sick, etc.)
- Living the life of a servant

Keep your lamps lit at all times. As the Word of God says, "You are the light for the world." *How do you keep your lamps lit at all times?*

John 11:9-10
Jesus said, a day has twelve hours, doesn't it? So those who walk in broad daylight do not stumble, for they see the light of this world. But if they walk during the night they stumble, because they have no light.

Acts 13:47
For this is the commandment that the Lord has given us: I have made you a light for the Gentiles, so that the entire world may be saved.

You get your lamps lit all the time by daily being in God's awesome presence. In His awesome presence, He anoints you all the time and provides you with daily bread to keep you for that particular day. He fills you up with His love to enable you to cope in your present life situation. He anoints your head with oil that strengthens you in your daily walk with Him. You have to go in the presence of the Lord every day to have an intimate relationship with Him. In this way, He tells you His perfect will and blesses you for that day you are in, as every day has its own encounters. Daily encountering God keeps your lamps lit at all times. In that way, you are always abreast of all changes.

You also get your lamps lit every time by listening to and doing what God has asked you to do. Be obedient to God's Word! God has commanded you to be faithful and loyal to Him, to proclaim His Word, and to make yourself visible to the world as His child.

Matthew 5:14-16
You are like light for the whole world. A city built on a hill cannot be hid. No one lights a lamp and puts it under a bowl; instead it is put on the lampstand, where it gives light for everyone in the house. In the same way your light must shine before people, so that they will see the good things you do and praise your Father in heaven.

Let your light shine in the dark places where no religion is. Let the world know of your light. Keep your lamps lit all the time for God's glory. Be a guiding light for the paths of the oppressed, lost, disadvantaged, sick, poor, persecuted, etc. Keeping your lights shining can only be done by listening to and keeping His Word in your heart through hard times—during times of confronting the Enemy, during times of strife, and during the darkest hour (the midnight hour).

The concepts of the parable of the virgins and the parable of the wedding feast are well understood when you are familiar with the wedding customs in the time of Christ. There are three distinct parts of the marriage.

The Betrothal

The betrothal ceremony changes the relationship status between the bride and the bridegroom. The bridegroom leaves the home of his father and travels to the home of the bride to obtain her for marriage. A marriage contract is then drawn up between the parents of the bride and the bridegroom. A bride price is then paid by the parents of the bridegroom to the bride or her parents.

The Preparation

In today's vernacular, this ceremonial part of the marriage is what would be called the engagement. The bride (*the church or the Bride of Christ*) was paid a bride price (*in the form of the blood of Jesus Christ on the cross*) by the bridegroom's parents. Inviting guests to the royal banquet at the end of this world was *the initiation period.* They come together as one in the Lord. The **preparation period** is when the Lord comes to prepare the bride for the day of the banquet. This period addresses the death of Christ on the cross, when He established a marriage covenant between Himself and the Church. The bridegroom then leaves for the Father's house again to prepare a place for them to live after the actual wedding ceremony (*the ascension of Christ).*

The Expectation Period

The ten virgins in the parable were in this phase of the marriage ceremony, waiting and watching for the bridegroom to return from His journey to take the bride (the church) to the home that He has prepared.

The Actual Marriage Ceremony

This ceremony usually takes place a year later when the bridegroom with his male friends went to the house of the bride at midnight with a torchlight parade through the street. The bride (the Church) would know this was going to take place and would be prepared along with her maidens (the workers in the field) to join the parade when the time comes. This parade would end up at the home prepared by the bridegroom, symbolizing the coming of Christ into the world to capture His faithful servants to His Father's house.

The Marriage Supper

The marriage supper, which is yet to come, is illustrated by the wedding in Cana in the Gospel of John 2:1-12. It is the final step (the resurrection of the church).

What John saw in the Book of Revelation throws light on the wedding feast of the lamb (Christ) and His bride (the Church) to come. The betrothal and the actual wedding stages are here with us already. The calling to the banquet has already been done after Christ died on the cross and signed that contract with us in His blood. When He was on the cross, we were called to the wedding banquet at the end of this world. Preparation is being made to look forward to the day that He will return to take us back to His Father's home.

Being devoted to Jesus, His Word, and works is the ultimate answer because lamps without oil will be left out of the parade and will not make it to the resurrection of the saints and the triumphant entry. Those with lamps void of oil will not be well-dressed for the entry because they will be clothed in the wrong clothing. The clothing of righteousness is needed to make it to the kingdom gates; those without the right clothing will not be able to enter. Jerusalem gates will be closed on you.

The right cloth! The right entry!

The triumphal entry is the key to succeeding in accessing the kingdom.

The Parable of the Virgins (Matthew 25:1-13)

The parable of the virgins illustrates the preparation for the Second Coming of Christ. This parable demonstrates waiting for the bridegroom to come and carry the bride with Him to His Father's home. But the waiting is the problem; many things can happen between the waiting period and His coming. Being prepared and staying prepared is the key.

The ten virgins in the parable represent the maidens of the bride (*the workers in the field*) waiting for the bridegroom to come.

At that time the Kingdom of heaven will be like this. Once there were ten young women who took their oil lamps and went out to meet the bridegroom. Five of them were foolish, and the other five were wise. The foolish ones took their lamps but did not take any extra oil with them, while the wise ones took containers full of oil for their lamps. The bridegroom was late in coming, so they began to nod and fall asleep.

It was already midnight when the cry rang out, Here is the bridegroom! Come and meet him! The ten young women woke up and trimmed their lamps. Then the foolish ones said to the wise ones, let us have some of your oil, because our lamps are going out. No, indeed, the wise ones answered, there is not enough for you and for us. Go to the store and buy some for yourselves. So the foolish ones went off to buy some oil; and while they were gone, the bridegroom arrived. The five who were ready went in with him to the wedding feast, and the door was closed. Later the others arrived. Sir, sir! Let us in! they cried out. Certainly not! I don't know you, the bridegroom answered. And Jesus concluded, Watch out, then, because you do not know the day or the hour (Matthew 25:1-13).

V. 1: Once there were ten young women who took their oil and went out to meet the bridegroom. This is the epilogue of what the passage is all about and refers to the second stage of the marriage customs.

Vv. 2-4: The maidens reacted when they heard a cry out at midnight that the bridegroom was on his way—sending out letters. The bridegroom was already running late, so the maidens began to nod and fell asleep.

V. 7: The maidens woke up to the cry and trimmed their lamps. They weren't sleeping deeply for them to hear the cry—unless some were light sleepers and awakened the others.

Vv. 3, 4, 8-10: The problems of the awakening lie in these verses:
- ✓ The preparation period (vv. 3, 4)
- ✓ The waiting period (v. 5)
- ✓ The expectation period (vv. 6-12)
- ✓ The warning (v. 13)

The Preparation Period

The ten young women are in the vineyard, working for the Lord in building His kingdom of rest. The vineyard is large and needs more workers. The young women are anointed with His Spirit to do His work. They are the reproductive system of the Church— the ones building the Church to the size required. They are virgins with pure hearts, needing circumcision.

Working through the vineyard idolizes them, and as workers, some of them took God's work for granted while others idolized it. They messed around doing His work until they heard His Son coming for His bride, the Church. They were not prepared for the waiting and the coming. The foolish ones among them took no extra oil for their lamps, but the wise ones took extra containers of oil for their lamps. The wise ones were well-prepared.

The Waiting

The bridegroom (Christ) is running late in coming, so the young women have lingered around while the bridegroom is on His way. Due to the unexpected delay of the bridegroom, the young women begin to nod and fall asleep. They grew tired of waiting, which normally happens in a waiting period.

During the waiting period, one must gird their loins and not fall into temptation. Wait on the Lord to come through for you. One must be humble and put on the cloth of righteousness for the triumphant entry.

The Expectation

The bridegroom will call at midnight when you least expect Him—when you are nodding and falling asleep. He will come unannounced like a thief in the night. Midnight, the middle of the night, represents the darkest hour in your life when things are unbearable. Then the Son of God will come and rescue you to His Father's home. At that time, the Enemy, the Devil will be at work, causing havoc in the world and the Church. You will either give in to the Enemy's work or stand by the Lord and worship Him.

The ten young women woke up to trim their lamps, implying that they could not stay awake all night waiting and watching. The foolish ones found themselves with no oil, and their lamps went out. They had no oil in their lamps because the anointing that was given to them was taken away from them due to deceit, unbelief, and unfaithfulness. The anointing on them will be no more because they did not do any work to keep it flowing in them.

They will not go in the presence of the Lord every day for their daily bread—their combat power to rekindle their light. Their lamps will go out and finally, when the keeper of the vineyard (the bridegroom, Christ) comes, He will not find them ready. They would not be properly dressed in their cloth of righteousness, and their light would be out because of their lack of devotion to the Lord. They would yield nothing in the fields.

The foolish ones woke to the cry of His coming and requested the wise ones to share their oil with them but they said, "No, go and fetch your own." Salvation is for each individual and not for the many. A person may only seek salvation for himself and no one else. You cannot save someone who is not ready to be saved. The path to salvation is long and needs interaction to get there—not isolation. You cannot isolate yourself from the Word of God to make that journey. The vineyard is large with lots of work to be done on it; go and cultivate your own. Touch the hearts of men and share the Word of God; this is what the wise ones do for themselves.

The five foolish virgins left to buy oil for their lamps, but on their return, they found that the bridegroom had already taken with Him the five wise ones, who had prepared for His coming to the feast and had closed the door to the banquet (feast). Once the Lord closes a door, no one can open it; *the door to salvation will be shut.*

The door to salvation is wide and untimely. To allow you to enter through the door, the lifespan of salvation is long for your sake. God has given you the privilege to enter through the door. He has thrown out the invitation to the Church and has given you ample time to sort out your heart about salvation. Once He closes the door to salvation, it is closed forever; no one can open it.

The Warning

And Jesus concluded, watch out, then, because you do not know the day or the hour.

- What do you do on the "watch out"?

You honor the Lord with the following:

- Humility
- Daily devotion
- Wearing the garment of righteousness

These three elements are needed to make a triumphant entry through the doors to the New Jerusalem for the wedding feast. The Day of the Lord's coming is drawing near, and we are about doing our own work. As no one knows the time or day of His coming, we must always have our cloth of righteousness on, should He come at any moment. This is the word of the Lord.

You must always be prepared!

Part Four

The Recipients

Friend, how did you get in here without wedding clothes? the king asked him. But the man said nothing. Then the king told the servants, tie him up hand and foot, and throw him outside in the dark. There he will cry and gnash his teeth.

And Jesus concluded, many are invited, but few are chosen.

- Matthew 22:12-14

Chapter Seven

The Banquet

The wedding banquet of the Lord has not yet taken place. It is waiting for your response to the invitation. The first stage—the bride price/engagement ceremony has been done. The second stage—the invitation to the banquet is here with us.

Jesus again used parables in talking to the people. The Kingdom of heaven is like this. Once there was a king who prepared a wedding feast for his son. He sent his servants to tell the invited guests to come to the feast, but they did not want to come. So he sent other servants with this message for the guests: My feast is ready now; my steers and prize calves have been butchered, and everything is ready. Come to the wedding feast! But the invited guests paid no attention and went about their business: one went to his farm, another to his store, while others grabbed the servants, beat them, and killed them. The king was very angry; so he sent his soldiers, who killed those murderers and burned down their city. Then he called his servants and said to them, my wedding feast is ready, but the people I invited did not deserve it. Now go to the main streets and invite to the feast as many people as you find. So the servants went out into the streets and gathered all the people they could find, good and bad alike; and the wedding hall was filled with people. The king went in to look at the guests and saw a man who was not wearing wedding clothes.

Friend, how did you get in here without wedding clothes? the king asked him. But the man said nothing. Then the king told the servants, tie him up hand and foot, and throw him outside in the dark. There he will cry and gnash his teeth.

And Jesus concluded, many are invited, but few are chosen (Matthew 22:1-14).

The invitations to the various guests called to the banquet have been sent out, but to whom and how were they sent? To enable us understand the whole preparation process, one needs to know what the banquet involves. Jesus says the kingdom of Heaven is like a king who prepared a wedding feast for a **son** and sent his servants to tell **the invited guests** to come to the feast, but they did not want to come. So, he sent out other servants with this **message** for the guests.

Who is involved in the wedding feast?

- The bride (the Church)
- The bridegroom (Christ)
- The king (God, the Father)
- The other invited guests

Who Are the Invited Guests?

The answer lies within Matthew 21:28-32; the parable of the sons.

The Invited Guests

The Parable of the Two Sons

Now, what do you think? There was once a man who had two sons. He went to the older one and said, Son, go and work in the vineyard today. I don't want to, he answered, but later he changed his mind and went. Then the father went to the other son and said the same thing. Yes, sir, he answered, but he did not go. Which one of the two did what his father wanted?

The older one, they answered. So Jesus said to them, I tell you: the tax collectors and the prostitutes are going into the Kingdom of God ahead of you. For John the

Baptist came to you showing you the right path to take, and you would not believe him; but the tax collectors and the prostitutes believed him. Even when you saw this, you did not later change your minds and believe him (Matthew 21:28-32).

Verse 28 of the chapter asks, *"Now, what do you think?"* This question is posed to the spiritual Jew who believes himself as the only one chosen for the banquet of the Lord but is forgetting that he has trespassed God's will. We become spiritual Jew by not accepting Christ (see Romans 2:25-29; Galatians 6:15-16; Ephesians 2:11-19). For years, you have been waiting for the Messiah and still waiting, but you will not see Him until the end. Why? Because you are the unbeliever in Christ; you have accepted God's Word but do not believe in Jesus Christ as His Son, the Messiah to come. Although you believe in God's Word, you do not believe in the message that Christ is preaching.

Jesus is preaching the message of love to the churches, which is the resurrection message and the message to bring us out of this distress—*the Messianic message*. His banner over us is love.

- You do not see "love" as the savior of this world?

If you do, then you see the Lord Jesus Christ as the Messiah to this world and the Church. **"The Messiah shall come but in His humble state to mankind."** Although God presented His Son, Jesus Christ to you, you still do not believe in Him.

You do not believe in love as the Savior of the Church and this world—the reason you still doubt and fight against His presence among us. Jesus is love! You never thought the Messiah would come in His humble state as He did, born in a stable and lay in a manger. "Humble beginning comes great things" according to the parable of the mustard seed (Matthew 13:31-35).

The question asked is for the spiritual Jew who believes the Messiah has not yet come and still waiting for His coming. The next question is: "Now, what do you think of the two sons in the parable?"

- Jesus is asking you for your opinion of Him.
- What is your mind telling you?
- He wants you to convict yourself.
- The question is, "Did you convict yourself, and how?"

The answer is No! You are still embracing your unbelief mentality after receiving your invitation to the banquet in the parable of the wedding feast.

But the invited guests paid no attention and went about their business: one went to his farm, another to his store (Matthew 22:5).

You still go on about your business and cannot make room for God. This is like you—always busy doing what you do, that you tend to forget about your purpose on this earth—*the purpose of your living.*

You reject Jesus, making excuses not to follow Him or listen to His message. You rely on your strength for everything, but not on God's strength.

Observing the characters of the two sons

(c.f. Hebrews 8:13; Romans 10:2-4)

The Elder Son (vv. 28-29)

He went to the older one and said, Son, go and work in the vineyard today. I don't want to, he answered, but later he changed his mind and went.

He was stubborn at heart, but later got convicted by the preaching of the message of repentance because the message had been implanted in his heart. However, stubbornness stopped him from heeding to the message. He said *no* to going and working in the vineyard. Later, he repented and obeyed his father's word in working in His vineyard.

Although in the beginning, he refused to obey his father and went about doing his business. He was honest with Him in not working in His vineyard. These are the scribes, Pharisees, and other self-righteous people.

The Other Son (v. 30)

Then the father went to the other son and said the same thing. Yes, sir, he answered, but he did not go.

The other son, on the other hand, showed the character of deception, faithfulness, and obedience in one context, but he did not heed to his father's call. This is very confusing, having both deception and faithfulness in the same context. He knew the word, what to do with it and what was expected of him, but he turned his back on the word. You lying to the Lord about your willingness to go and your non-adherence to His will are pure deceit. **"Faith with no works is dead."**

Why does the elder son regret his disobedience?

The son was reluctant in the beginning to change, but the vicissitudes of life made him change his mind (read Job 24:1-25; Lamentation 3:27; Romans 8:7) and heed to the father's calling. The son regretted his actions of disobedience due to society's peer pressure. He lived in a society where everyone classified him as the unacceptable, but the Lord accepted him just as he was, because the door to salvation has no measurement. Regardless, it is wide enough to accommodate anybody. He changed because he had nowhere else to go or no one else to turn to but the Father. He accepted his mistakes and decided to turn away from peer pressure.

He made a critical decision about his salvation and took a step of faith toward it, which is not easy to do. For him to take the step of faith, he had to believe in the One to whom he was turning—A BIG DECISION! He changed because disobedience made him lack many things in the Lord. He changed according to the way the Word was preached to him by the messenger.

He changed because he wanted to make something good out of his life. He disobeyed the Father because he did not have any choice in the world in which he lives. His life was already ruined and nothing better could be made from it. He was perfectly incapable of rescuing himself from his dead self.

He moved from the state of incapability to a state of capability by repenting and accepting Jesus Christ as his Lord and Savior. He made something with his life which before had been impossible. He was on the right path to righteousness to be saved (Luke 7:29; Ezekiel 18:30-32; Acts 3:19; Romans 2:4-11).

Why does the other son fail to be obedient?

This answer is the main reason for the parable—**UNBELIEF**. God is talking about the UNBELIEF in you. You tend to talk about the unbelievable things of God although you yourself do not believe. You do not understand the things of God while pretending you do, in most cases. You vividly illustrate the things of God, but you do not understand how it came about. You tend not to understand the concept of what God does.

God has sent His messengers, John the Baptist, and His Son, Jesus Christ, to you. One to show you the way (the right path to Him), and the other to deliver you from the sins of the world and baptize you into His holy calling.

- But what did you do with them?

You turn them away as outcasts and believe in your own righteousness. You render them useless in their state and tend to your old ways. You listen to gossip and lies about the word, but not to the Word of God. You turn away from the Lord instead of turning to Him. You make your way impossible while it is possible. You divert His Word into something unbearable but meanwhile it is bearable.

For the yoke I will give you is easy, and the load I will put on you is light (Matthew 11:30).

You make something out of nothing. You reduce His Word to nothing, coming up with your own word. You make jokes about Him and slander Him. You are the princes of the land; you deserve to be treated as such. You deserve to be highly exalted, but you are not. You go about your daily life as if you are in charge of your own life, although the Lord is. You cannot live if God does not allow you to.

He is the Master of your life, and as such, you must acknowledge Him. Treat Him with respect; do not mock or lay acquisitions on Him. He is God.

In Matthew 21:28-32, the elder son appeared obedient in the beginning when he was asked to go to the vineyard to work. When the eldest son was asked at first, he had a belief in his father. But as time passed, his belief system changed as the world closed in on him. He appeared obedient, but deceit made him reluctant to obey the Father's word when the time came for him to go. This reluctance is an indication of

unbelief on his part. He lost everything because of **unbelief** and **deceit.** He changed from being obedient to disobedient. (Read Matthew 23:25-26; Job 8:13, 27:8-12; Luke 6:45; Galatians 5:19-23).

The Warning (vv. 31-32)

Due to your unbelief, you will miss out on the feast because without "belief," you cannot meet God's requirements that qualify you for the feast—*being dressed in the right clothing.* You must be prepared for the feast, and the preparation involves getting ready for the coming of Christ. It involves commitment to the Lord and in order to be committed, you must have faith in Him, which comes by hearing His Word and believing in Him.

Without faith, you cannot serve Him as you should. You are a lukewarm Christian who does things to please men rather than God. You are a hypocrite or worse. Your belief has to be 100 percent to be able to meet His demands, but you are a lukewarm Christian and always looking for a good opportunity to ditch Him. You always look for excuses not to worship Him while you can. The modern Christian is perplexed with certain matters. You are in this modern-age world; however, the time you are in, is a time of great achievements in which things are being touched by the Holy Spirit, but not by your own strength.

The Holy Spirit is doing so much work in your life that you tend to forget your Creator. You are in lust with worldly things, which have clouded your mind because of what it provides you. They have become your priority in your daily life. You live by it, breathe it, and are enslaved by worldliness.

Heaven and earth will pass away, but my words will never pass away (Mark 13:31).

Worldly things are beautiful and interesting, but the price you pay for them is excruciating. **Live by His Word and slave by His Word!** Jesus is talking to the unbelieving Christian, who always looks down upon the unsaved, thinking less of them, but strictly speaking, you, the unbelieving Christian, are the worst of all. Because of your unbelief and hypocritical lifestyle, the Book of Matthew said, "*The last shall be the first and the first shall be the last.*"

And Jesus concluded, so those who are last will be first, and those who are first will be last (Matthew 20:16).

Jesus was talking about how you will be the last to enter the kingdom of God due to your unbelief and make the unsaved the first to enter due to their repentance, belief, and sincerity.

He will only let the good ones in and let the bad ones stay outside the door with the enemy. They will stay outside together because of the covenant to live in each other's life.

The kingdom of god is of good faith.

Who was invited?

How were they invited?

What was their response to the invitation?

Invited guest?

The Parable of the Tenants in the Vineyard (Matthew 21:33-46)

Listen to another parable, Jesus said. There was once a landowner, who planted a vineyard, put a fence around it, dug a hole for the wine press, and built a watchtower. Then he rented the vineyard to tenants and left home on a trip. When the time came to gather the grapes, he sent his slaves to the tenants to receive his share of the harvest. The tenants grabbed his slaves, beat one, killed another, and stoned another. Again the man sent other slaves, more than the first time, and the tenants treated them the same way. Last of all he sent his son to them. Surely they will respect my son, he said. But when the tenants saw the son, they said to themselves, this is the owner's son. Come on, let's kill him, and we will get his property! So they grabbed him, threw him out of the vineyard, and killed him.

Now, when the owner of the vineyard comes, what will he do to those tenants? Jesus asked. He will certainly kill those evil men, they answered, and rent the vineyard out to other tenants, who will give him his share of the harvest at the right time.

Jesus said to them, Haven't you ever read what the Scriptures say? The stone which the builders rejected as worthless turned out to be the most important of all. This was done by the Lord; what a wonderful sight it is! And so I tell you, added Jesus, the Kingdom of God will be taken away from you and given to a people who will produce the proper fruits. The chief priests and the Pharisees heard Jesus' parables and knew that he was talking about them, so they tried to arrest him. But they were afraid of the crowds, who considered Jesus to be a prophet. (Matthew 21:33-46)

The vineyard has been rented to you and me to cultivate and yield grapes (souls) for the winepress when the time comes.

What is a tenant?

- (noun) Entity that (1) occupies or possesses a property by any type of claim, right, or title, or (2) pays periodic rent for a temporary right to occupy, possess, and/or use a property; the right having been granted by the property owner (landlord) through a lease or tenancy agreement.

What are the duties of a tenant?

Tenants, as well as landlords, also have certain obligations they must follow under landlord-tenant law. The main obligations of tenants based on the type of tenancy are:

- Adhering to the tenancy agreement
- Maintaining the property
- Allowing the landlord access to the property

The rights and responsibilities of the tenant will be detailed in the tenancy agreement which both parties have to sign.

What are the safety issues of a tenant?

Primarily, it is the landlord's duty to make sure the property is safe, but there are some things the tenant can do to protect themselves such as:

- learn about the crime statistics of the area
- Take note of the safety condition of the property.

The main points of the parable are as follows:

- The tenant refuses to attend to the vineyard; therefore, he or she has no grapes for the landowner. You miraculously beat, killed, and stoned the slaves God sent to you.
- They turned down the offer to cultivate the vineyard.
- They left it unattended with the full responsibility of not tending to it.

- They then murdered the slaves God sent and hid their innocence.

What message did the slaves carry?
- They carried the message of repentance, salvation, and restoration.
- The third time, God sent His Son (*representing Jesus Christ*) to the world, but we seized Him, threw Him out of the vineyard, and killed Him. Killing Him made Him the chief cornerstone of the vineyard.
- You exalted Him instead of bringing Him down.
- You made Him King over them.
- You rejected Him, but He became King in the end.

Not all refused to cultivate the vineyard; some did, but the majority among them did not.
- God sent the message round through His prophets at that time, telling you about His will. He sowed His seed (the Word) for His kingdom building in you and waited for it to be harvested in the right season. The seed grew, but not all of it yielded a fruit—*fruitless bearing tree* (referring to the parables of the sower, the talents, and the gold coin).

Some yielded fruits according to their ability, and some did not. The spread of the Word got hindered by our fleshly desires and ungodly purposes. We rebuked God's Word and made a laughing stock of Him.

The parable deals with **decency** (*the quality of being polite and respectable*) and **respectability** toward God and His Word.

V. 40: Jesus is asking a powerful question—a question that would bring a realization to yourself.

When the owner of the vineyard comes, what will he do to those tenants? Jesus asked.

This is a question of **authenticity.** He wanted you to know what will happen at the end of this world. Out of curiosity, do you know that Jesus will win in the end? Have you not read the Scriptures that the Father will not destroy the earth again with flood but with His inextinguishable fire (Holy Ghost fire)?

V. 42: *Jesus said to them, Haven't you ever read what the Scriptures say? The stone which the builders rejected as worthless turned out to be the most important of all. This was done by the Lord; what a wonderful sight it is!*

The stone that you are casting away as being worthless will one day be the stone through which your salvation will come. He shall be the cornerstone, and without Him, you would be worth nothing.

V. 43: *And so I tell you, added Jesus, the Kingdom of God will be taken away from you and given to a people who will produce the proper fruits.*

God will not let the vineyard out to other tenants, but He will take it away from you and give it to someone who will recognize or appreciate Him as God, respecting Him through His Son. That someone will acknowledge His Son, Jesus Christ and be a doer of the Word that He preaches to you, which is **SALVATION.**

How were the guests invited? (cf. Revelation 2-3; Luke 17:20-37)

In medieval times, invitations were sent out to invitees by hand through agents or servants. The invitations were sent out through the servants of God—*the medium through which He operates*—to the prospective candidates by the bridegroom's family. The invitees (*the selected few*) are handpicked by the groom's family.

The invitation has been sent to us.

- Have you responded to yours?
- Did you accept or refuse His invitation?

The invitation has been sent to all ends of the world at three different times.

The Invitation

First Invitation

The first invitation went out to Adam and Eve in the Garden of Eden, but the invitation was turned down by accepting the fruit from the serpent.

- *Why did God represent their deceit by a fruit?*

He made man out of nothing, but soil. He stroked them from the ground, and they shared what He specifically asked them not to do in His church: deception.

The fruit (*a fruit is a product of a tree or other plant that contains seed*) stands for deception and cunningness because of how beautiful the tree is and how good its fruit will be like to eat—just as the Devil in his camouflaged clothing deceives you. That is why the Lord is asking you to be on your guard against the Pharisees and the Sadducees; they have been made like the forbidden fruit of the tree and hand them out to culprits who are unwise to eat them. Temptations are on the earth; as such, you must take good care of yourself as a child of God.

You reject God as your head. Life is becoming very unpleasant on earth because you are living a life of deceit as people created in God's image and likeness. You deceive Him and lead an adulterous life (worshipping other gods, including money).

But first he must suffer much and be rejected by the people of this day. As it was in the time of Noah so shall it be in the days of the Son of Man. Everybody kept on eating and drinking, and men and women married, up to the very day Noah went into the boat and the flood came and killed them all (Luke 17:25-27).

Second Invitation

Another invitation went out a second time, and you still failed to respond to the invite. Some of you did respond and the others did not.

It will be as it was in the time of Lot. Everybody kept on eating and drinking, buying and selling, planting and building. On the day Lot left Sodom, fire and sulphur rained down from heaven and killed them all. **That is how it will be on the day the Son of Man is revealed** (Emphasis added, Luke 17:28-30).

On that day someone who is on the roof of a house must not go down into the house to get any belongings; in the same way anyone who is out in the field must not go back to the house. Remember Lot's wife! Those who try to save their own life will lose it; those who lose their life will save it. On that night, I tell you, there will be two people sleeping in the same bed: one will be taken away, the other will be left behind. Two women will be grinding meal together: one will be taken away, the other will be left behind. The disciples asked him, Where, Lord? Jesus answered, Wherever, there is a dead body, the vultures will gather (Luke 17:31-37).

Fire and sulfur rained down and destroyed them all. The remnant shall return! Two things happened here: fire and sulfur rained down from heaven, and they were killed by the very thing that was to save them. That is the story of the fire and the sulfur. Sulfur does not kill but eliminates you from the earth. The fire is to protect you, but now it has turned against you. The fire of the Lord is for us, but we are playing with that fire. God will rain the fire on us on Pentecost Day.

- The fire reached us but in what state were we?

The fire touches our soul and purifies us but the harm is done when the purification is turned into hatred. The Lord will use what was meant to save us to kill us. He is the Lord with the two-edged sword in His mouth. He can claim us to Himself, and at the same time, He can give us up. The salt of sulfur will rain on us if we refuse to worship Him in truth. He will forsake us and bring us to judgment in His house.

The salt of sulfur will burn us; so does the fire of God. He will disintegrate us from the earth. His water will not flood the earth again to wash us from our sins, but His judgment will come upon us through His fire and the salt of sulfur which will disintegrate us from the earthly realm.

Third Invitation

This invitation went out when Jesus Christ was born into this world as a child, with John the Baptist preaching repentance and the need to be baptized with water. Jesus Christ died on the cross to open the door to salvation. The door is wide and allows anyone in, so who are you to tell someone they are not fit to be saved? The door allows anyone in, excluding nobody. It does not discriminate; the restrictions were taken off, allowing everyone in, regardless of how sinful the person is. There is a chance to repent and accept Jesus Christ as your Savior. Through Him, you will be accepted into God's kingdom to enjoy the feast of the wedding.

Jesus looked at them and asked, what, then, does this scripture mean? The stone which the builders rejected as worthless turned out to be the most important of all. Everyone who falls on that stone will be cut to pieces; and if that stone falls on someone, that person will be crushed to dust (Luke 20:17-18).

In the early Christian times, the invitations were sent to seven churches in the province of Asia to reproach their behavior. Jesus opened the way to salvation for you, giving you the liberty to go to the cross, repent of your sin and take up the heavy cross. All the messages were sent out after Christ was born as a child; now He is to come to us as a Son, giving us the privilege to come and worship God. Therefore, the third calling is all about **salvation and restoration**, which is being done through the feeding of the five thousand through Jesus' disciples (that is you).

The Seven Churches

The seven churches represent the community of worshippers living in each city, not entirely a church building. These are the seven types of worship in the Body of Christ today—the Seven Churches of the Lampstand. God spoke to the Church about His lampstand.

Ephesus: This church had a touch for God, but had forsaken God, her first love (Revelations 2:4).

Smyrna: This church had no sense of where it was going, no sense of direction. This church would suffer punishment from the Father for its wickedness (Revelations 2:10).

Pergamon: This church had lost track of everything ever owned and had no sense of how to track it back. This is the time you need maturing. It represents all stages of life. This church needs repentance from the Lord (Revelation 2:16).

Thyatira: This church made a lot of mistakes in his life (in maturing) and didn't know how to go back to the Lord for forgiveness and direction. You made a lot of mistakes in maturing to faith. This church had a false prophetess as their god (Revelation 2:20).

Sardis: This church had something in hand but did not know how to redeem it. They have been positioned to win but do not know how to go about it in order to win. This church had fallen asleep (Revelation 3:2).

Philadelphia: This church had everything given to them. You have made it to the cross but feel <u>no obligation</u> to worship the Father. Some feel reluctant not to worship the Father; it is understandable. When the time comes, you should not call on Him to defend you. That will be the end of time—*the end-time church*. This church has endured patiently.

Laodicea: This church is composed of pitiful ones who had it all, but messed it up journeying toward the Promised Land. This church had a lukewarm faith (Revelation 3:16).

These are the people God wants to save from, the Enemy. He has set up His lampstand; the seven churches in equal rights to reach you from all ends and make God available to you as you cry out to Him.

The invitation has gone out to the seven churches in the province of Asia as a representation of their Christian faith in the world. God represented His guests to the banquet with the seven churches in the province of Asia, which tells you about how bad these churches are in His eyes. He has presented them to you to see how bad you are doing in terms of love and how desperate He is to rescue you from your sin and bring you to restoration.

The Lampstand and the Church

The Church defines the Lampstand and its structure. The Church tells you the reason behind the construction and existence. It constitutes the reason God is among His people and why His people are with Him. The Church is deviating from its traditional principles and taking up principles that do not coincide with its beliefs. The Church principles are dying, and in as much as the Church is kept alive, its principles are dying. The Lampstand does not talk about anything but the principles of the Church to come back. It stands for the Church and the things that the Church will have to go through before it achieves its principles right.

The Church is the soul of God and in His soul is the Church. You cannot distinguish one from the other. The Church is within Christ and Christ is within the Church. You cannot tear them apart. The Church has to be together in order to pass the Father's will. At the moment, the Church is divided. The Church cannot be torn apart. It has to stay together to bring about the perfect end. Taking a look at the construction of the lampstand, God instructed that the pure gold be beaten together to form unison. It was not beaten into pieces, then put together. They were engineered together as one piece. As much as we want the church to be the perfect place of restoration, we cannot do that without the light of God. We need His light to bring us out and restore us.

The light of the Lord is Jesus Christ. The base and shaft of the lampstand were hammered out first; the base then the shaft, before the six branches. The shaft of the lampstand is Jesus Christ, but the base is the principles of God's word on which the Church is built upon. The base is the foundation of the Church and upon that foundation is Jesus Christ. The Church is birthed out of the sufferings of the Lord Jesus Christ. He is the center of the Church. The sufferings of Christ indicate what the Church will go through to bring that perfection to the Church. The sufferings of the Church tell you the future of the Church. The churches within the Church are to share in His sufferings.

Make a lampstand of pure gold. Make its base and its shaft of hammered gold; its decorative flowers, including buds and petals, are to form one piece with it. Six branches shall extend from its sides, three from each side. (Exodus 25:31-32)

Exodus 25:31-32 talks about that piece of construction where the pure gold was hammered out first to construct the base and then the shaft of the lampstand. They then went on to construct the six branches extending from the hammered shaft. Although we are in Christ, our sufferings are with Christ. We live in Him and Him in us. The Church can never do without Christ, because in Him we live. We are bound together in Christ as one. We cannot live or survive without Christ. He is our foundation and life. Christ was bound together with the Church. The Church shares in His sufferings, so do we share in His righteousness. You cannot separate Christ from the Church.

The Lampstand stands for the churches in the Church. Do not bring division in the Church as that is not of God's mission. His mission is to unite the Church as one unit in His name. Therefore, the representation of the Church with the menorah; God's oneness in us.

Therefore, the mystery behind the presence of the Lampstand as part of the furniture in the holy place shows that it binds the churches together as one. It weaves the churches together as one. The Lampstand is to bring light to our situation and enlighten the Church about who God is from the beginning. It shone the light on the Church as to who God is and how He is going to bring them out of their situation. God created a way for the churches and that way is through the sufferings of His only begotten Son.

It is only through the sufferings of Jesus Christ will the Church be saved. Christ suffered the way He did for the Church to share in His suffering. It is a symbol of what the Church has to go through in order to be saved. The principles of the Church lie within the Church.

The construction of the tabernacle is to bring love among God's people; the entire region of the land. That is His main reason—to love us as we should be and dedicate Christ to us on earth. That is His entire reason for coming to us on earth; to show His love to us. Christ suffered for the Church, so does the Church suffer for the love of Christ. The six churches are the extension of Christ.

The dedication of the Church to Christ

This is what Mary went with the world when she was pregnant with the word. She dedicated herself to the word and brought out of herself Jesus, the king of the Jews.

Salvation is the word that is needed for the Church at this moment.

The seven churches exhibit every sin in God's Book which He dislikes. He does not stand for disobedience, unrighteousness, pride, deceit, inequality, discrimination, unforgiveness, ungratefulness, and resentment or rejection. The Father has sent His seven stars to the seven churches with the invitation letter. You have the opportunity to change according to His Word. These are the churches God has set up in unison by the beating of the pure gold. Still, the Devil is quickly destroying them by his own devious ways—turning the Church against God and making it change its ideas (principles) of Church, i.e., *ideology*.

Chapter Eight

The Invitation Message

What was the invitation message sent out?

The message in the second and third chapters of the Book of Revelation is an invitation to the Lord's Supper. The invitation highlighted the individual churches' fault(s) as it goes along. It likewise contains your mistakes and highlights them according to your need as the Father ministers to you individually—not as a group. You will find that His Word targets you individually and not as a group because God has a different word or assignment for each one of us. Your assigned message will not be the same as that of the other. The invitation highlights the following:

- Who is He to you as the Lord of Host?
- Your shortcoming(s)
- How God will help you through your shortcomings or punish you as a result of them
- Your reward in turning away from your sin

The Message

Nicolaitans

Nicolaism (Nicolaitanism) is a Christian heresy first mentioned twice in the second chapter of Revelation. The Nicolaitans are known in the cities of Ephesus and Pergamum.

- Ephesus was commended for her hatred of the deeds of the Nicolaitans.
- Pergamum, on the other hand, is blamed for embracing those who hold to Nicolaitan doctrines.

The Nicolaitans lead lives of unrestricted indulgence. They eat things offered to idols and allow multiple men to marry a wife. They support either polygamy or the holding of wives in common.

Nico means "conquer" in Greek and *laitan* refers to "lay people"; hence, the word may be taken to mean "lay conquerors" or "conquerors of the lay people."

Ephesus Message (Revelation 2:1-7)

The church is full of corruption and deceit. It is made of thieves.

Identity

The Lord identifies Himself as *"The One who holds the seven stars in his right hand and who walks among the seven gold lampstands."*

Representing
- Judgment
- He judges the seven churches using the seven stars in His right hand.
- He weighs them in His right hand to indicate what they are doing right or wrong.
- He assesses you accordingly.

Commendation
- Hardworking
- Patient
- Cannot tolerate evil people
- You have tested those who say they are apostles but are not, and found out that they are liars.
- Suffered for the Lord's sake, and has not given up
- Hated Nicolaitans' deeds as He does

The Accused
- You do not love Him as you did at first due to pollutions from other doctrines and the persecutions that you have suffered.

Recommendation

- Think about how far you have fallen!
- Go back to the beginning and see what you used to do and no longer do that anymore.
- Assess your way of living now and compare it to the past.
- Turn from your sins and do what you did at first, that is, **love the Father as you once did**.

Punishment

If you do not repent and turn away from your sins, the Father will take His glory (the lampstand) from you.

The Reward

To those who win the victory, He will give the right to eat the fruit of the Tree of Life that grows in His garden.

- You will gain intimate access to the Lord again.
- He took that right from you when you sinned in the Garden of Eden.
- You will have direct access to God through His Son, Jesus Christ.

(See Ezekiel 28:24-26).

Smyrna Message (Revelation 2:8-11)

The days of your strife are over. You received a letter of invitation to the Lord's salvation party but did you receive it with gladness?

Identity

He is the One who is the first and the last, who died and lived again (Revelation 1:17-18).

- The beginning and the end (He was at the beginning of the world and will be at the end of this world.)
- The Alpha and Omega
- The Resurrection and the Life
- The Conqueror of death
- The Holder of the key to life

Commendation

- You are poor, but really, you are rich!
- Evil things have been said about you by those who claim to be Jews but are not.

Recommendation

- Do not be afraid of anything for which you are about to suffer.
- He gave you an advance warning of the plans of the Devil, but He reassured you not to be afraid because He knows what He has in store for you afterward.
- He told you that the suffering won't last forever but will last for ten days.
- Be faithful to Him, He says, even if it means death (Luke 17:32).

The Reward

- He will reward you with life—if you die in His name. He is the giver of life.
- You will not be hurt by the second death.
  (See Revelation 2:8; Isaiah 44:6, 48:12; Revelation 1:17, 22:13; Revelation 20:14, 21:8).

Pergamum Message (Revelation 2:12-17)

The angel of the Lord sent a message to you to turn away from your sinful ways and make way to His cross. You are full of lust which God hates, and He wants to bring you out and show you love to oppose your lust.

- But did you accept the invitation?

No, you didn't. You chose a life as a lustful people in God because you lived among lustful people.

Identity

- He is the One who has the sharp two-edged sword (Revelation 1:16).
- His Word sanctifies the soul, and at the same time, rejuvenates the body.
- It can make or unmake you—just as the fig tree withered away by His word and the withered hand was restored by His word.

Commendation

- He knows where you live and where Satan has his throne.
- You are true to Him.
- You did not abandon your faith in Him even when Antipas, His faithful witness, was killed where Satan lives.

Accused

- Some of you follow the teaching of Balaam, who taught Balak how to lead the people of Israel into sin by persuading you to eat food that has been offered to idols and to practice sexual immorality.
- You have people among you who follow the teaching of the Nicolaitans.

Recommendation

- Now, turn from your sins!
- This is a strong warning to you.

Punishment

- If you do not turn from your sins, He will come to you soon and fight against you with the sword that comes from His mouth.
- If you have ears, then listen to what the Spirit is saying to the churches!

The Reward

- To those who win the victory, He will give:
  - Some of the hidden manna, which is food for the hungry
- Each of you is a white stone representing His name, which is exclusive to the one God presents to you. In times of need, it is what He is to you; He will be your God. On that stone is written a new name that no one knows except the one who receives it. Because He is different to people in different ways and different circumstances, so He will appear to them differently.
- Based on your faith in Him, the new name reflects His identity on you.
- The new name He has given you will change your identity.
- Life in abundance (Read Revelation 2:14; Numbers 22: 5, 7, 31:16, 25:1-3; Deuteronomy 23:4; Exodus. 16:14-15, 33-34; John 6:48).

Thyatira Message (Revelation 2:18-29)

The message addresses the way you worship. You worship God in a way that discredits Him. You are idol worshippers and make your way as if you are a God-loving person. You worship Him in your heart and live your life as an idol worshipper. You eat their food and do everything that they do. In His eyes, they are mocking Him and making His Word as difficult as anything. They make Him impossible and unbelievable. They are the givers of life, but they are not the Restorer of life in abundance.

Identity

He is the Son of God, whose eyes blaze like fire, whose feet shine like polished brass.

- The Lord's eyes blaze with fire. In this usage, the word *blaze* means "a light within the field of vision that is brighter than the brightness to which the eyes are adapted." His voice resonates with affinity and clarity.
- His feet shine like polished brass.

Commendation

- He knows what you do.
- He knows your love.
- He knows your faithfulness.
- He knows your service.
- He knows your patience.
- He knows that you are doing more than you did at first.

Accusation

- You have tolerated Jezebel, who calls herself a messenger of God.
- You are following her teachings straight into practicing sexual immorality and eating food that has been offered to idols.

Recommendation

- The Lord has given Jezebel time to repent of her sins, but she does not want to turn from her immorality.
- But the rest of you in Thyatira have not followed this evil teaching; you have not learned what the others call "the deep secrets of Satan." The Lord says that He will not put any burden on you. But until He comes, you **must** hold firmly to what you have.

Punishment

To Jezebel and Co., if you do not repent of your sins, He will:

- Throw her on a bed where she and those who are committing adultery with her will suffer terribly.
- Do this now unless you repent of the wicked things you do with her.
- Also kill her followers and all the churches will know that the Lord is the One who knows everyone's thoughts and wishes.
- He will repay each of you according to what you have done.

The Reward

To those who win the victory, who continue to the end to do what He wants as opposed to what I want, He will give the same authority that He received from His Father:

- He will give them authority over nations, to rule them with an iron rod and to break them into pieces like clay pots.
- He will also give them the morning star.

The greatest reward ever! If you have ears, then listen to what the Spirit says to the churches!

(Read Revelation 2:20, 23, 26-27; 1 Kings 16:31; 2 Kings 9:22, 30; Psalm 7:9; Jeremiah 17:10; Psalm 62:12; Psalm 2:8-9).

Interlude

That says the Lord:

"I am the one who holds the seven stars to the seven churches in my right hand. I do what I want with the stars, I can order them to punish, to give grace, to alter things, to divide and to eliminate things. I am the one with the two-edged sword in my mouth. I can turn it anyhow, it can judge (punish) or restore (bless). I know what I want and I will get it. Restoration is good and judgment is bad. Do not let me judge you for your sins (disobedience). I hold the keys to the grave and let people out when it pleases me.

I am the King of the world and as such I hold authority over principalities and demons.

I hold the key to salvation and I am allowing everyone in, as my Father has ordered me to do. I hold the key to life. I am the way, the truth, and the life. No one comes to the Father except through me."

Hosanna!! God is good in all things.

Sardis Message (Revelation 3:1-6)

Sardis is a province with great expectations. You have prospects, but the Devil has misled you, making you forget about your past and the person who brought you out of your past. You were legions with copious problems, and by the grace of God, He brought you out of them. You made sacrifices for Him and pledged not to go back on your word, but the old serpent, the Devil, has made you go back on your word. God is warning you about your attitude!

The church in Sardis is all about the modern-aged Church and its attitude.

Identity

He is the One who has the seven spirits of God and the seven stars. The seven spirits are His manifestations through the Holy Spirit. He manifests the way He wants to through the Holy Spirit and that manifestation shows who He is at that time. He manifests in the following seven different ways through His Spirit:

1. The Spirit of the Lord (1 Corinthians 6:19-20; Romans 8:9).
2. The Spirit of wisdom (James 1:5)

3. The Spirit of understanding (John 16:13)
4. The Spirit of counsel (John 14:16)
5. The Spirit of power
6. The Spirit of knowledge
7. The Spirit of the fear of the Lord

This is how you see Him.

Commendation

- He knows that you have a reputation of being alive, even though you are dead!
- A few in Sardis still have clean clothes. Clothed in white, you walk with Him because you are worthy to do so.

Recommendation

- Wake up and strengthen what you still have before it dies completely. I find that what you have done is not yet perfect in the sight of God.
- Remember, then, what you were taught (Matthew 24:43-44; Luke 12:39-40; Revelation 16:15) and what you heard. Obey it and turn from your sins.

Punishment

If you do not wake up, He will come upon you like a thief, and you will not know the time when He will come.

The Reward

Those who win the victory:

- Will be clothed like this in white (the robe of righteousness)
- He will not remove your name from the book of the living.
- In the presence of the Father and His angels, He will declare openly that you belong to Him (Revelation 3:5, 20:12; Exodus 32:32-33; Psalm 69:28; Matthew 10:32; Luke 12:8).

Philadelphia Message (Revelation 3:7-13)

The church was also given a warning about its worship of God. You worship God anyhow (this is about discipline in His Church). You cast aside God and do your own worshipping. You do not respect God in any way; you mock Him with your soulish deeds. But this shall all end soon when the Son comes. Church of pitiful, you live according to the will of your gods. The time has come for God to place judgment on you. Jesus will crash hard on you idol worshippers in His Father's Church, and make a living hell out of you. He has sent His harsh warnings. He is preparing His way to you in the Church. No mercy to anyone who fails my trials. The Philadelphia church is a modern-age Church, and this is a recent invitation to you.

Identity

He is the One who is **holy** and **true**. Truth comes from Him; He is the Truth (John 18:28-38).

He has the key that belonged to David, and when He opens a door, no one can close it; when He closes it, no one can open it.

He holds the key to life. He is the Almighty God, nothing surpasses Him. He is the Alpha and Omega, the beginning and the end of all creation as evidenced in the Book of Revelation. He is the I Am that I Am, the Holder of your life, and He opens opportunities and closes the door to your past.

Commendation

He knows what you do; He knows that you have a little power.

- You are following His teaching.
- You are faithful to Him.

Warning

- He is coming soon! Keep safe what you have, so that no one will rob you of your victory prize. HOLD FAST TO YOUR FAITH.
- He sends a warning to the group that belongs to Satan, who claim to be Jews but are not. He will make them come and bow down at your feet. They will all know that He loves you.

The Reward

1. He has opened a door in front of you, which no one can close.
   - He has opened an opportunity for you—an escape route which no one can close.
   - He has the key to life because He conquered death and has opened the door to life—the door to salvation.

2. Because you are keeping His command (His will, His law) to endure, He has also kept you safe from this time of trouble, which has come upon the world testing each one of you on earth.
   - He is reassuring and comforting you through your trials.
   - Keep holding on to your faith in Him till the end.
   - He is also keeping you safe from the wrath that has come upon the earth.

     Do not bring us to hard testing, but keep us safe from the Evil One (Matthew 6:13).

3. He will make them pillars, those who are victorious, in the temple of His Father, and you will never leave it.
   - He will write on them the name of His God and the name of the city of His God, the New Jerusalem, which will come down out of Heaven from His God.

- He will also write on them (pillars) His new name—the name of the new King of Jerusalem. The man who died and raised again, the Messiah, the King of all kings and the ruler of the earth. He is who He is and who He will be when He comes to you as the ruler of the earth.
(Read Isaiah 49:23, 60:14, 43:4, 62:2, 65:15; Revelation 21:2; Isaiah 22:22; Job 12:14).

- *Question: What will be His new name?*

His name will be the Ruler of the earth. If you have ears, then listen to what the Spirit says to the churches!

Laodicea Message (Revelation 3:14-22)

This is the church of the final times (end days)—the church full of corruption, deceit, and false preachers. It is tongue-lashing times, when things are upside down in the House of God; the Church, and no one can cope with life and its attributes. But the ones who can sustain all His lashings, separating the chaff from the grain (trials and tribulations) will make a feast out of His calling. God has called us to His service. **You are in the End-Time Church** where everything you have in the Church is going through a test. You will inherit His rich kingdom in His name.

You are surviving upon everything that you are going through; obeying God's rules and regulations by sticking to

His Word. You are fighting a good fight of faith! Well done, faithful servant!

The Kingdom of God is here! This is the final curtain call to salvation, and then the curtain will be closed. This is the final call out to all mankind to repent and to make way to the cross where salvation is waiting for you. **This is the last call for salvation.**

Identity

This is the message from the **Amen**, the **faithful**, and the **true witness**, who is the origin of all that God has created.

- The **true witness** to His Word (Proverbs 8:22-23; John 1:1-2).
- In the beginning of the world, "the Word" already existed.
- **The Amen** — "the hope of glory"
- *Amen* is "a confirmation that His will be done."
- You say *Amen* to confirm God's will—His promise, the hope of glory in your life.
- *Amen* literally means "the hope of glory" in Christ.
- *Amen* affirms your faith and hope in Him.
- *Amen* is "a salutation to your faith in Him."
- *Amen* is said or sung to express a wish that a prayer should be fulfilled.

In planning this, did I appear fickle? When I make my plans, do I make them from selfish motives, ready to say

*"Yes, yes" and "No, no" at the same time? As surely as God speaks the truth, my promise to you was not a "Yes" and a "No." For Jesus Christ, the Son of God, who was preached among you by Silas, Timothy, and myself, is not one who is "Yes" and "No." On the contrary, he is God's "Yes"; **for it is he who is the "Yes" to all of God's promises.** This is why through Jesus Christ our **"Amen" is said to the glory of God**.* (Emphasis added, 2 Corinthians 1:17-20).

- All of God's promises are "YEA" and "AMEN."
- The promises are all TRUE and HOPEFUL.

The entire Bible closes with an affirmation of His word *Amen*, i.e., "Thy will be done."

John, to the seven churches which are in Asia: Grace to you and peace from Him who is and who was and who is to come, and from the seven Spirits who are before His throne, and from Jesus Christ, the faithful witness, the firstborn from the dead, and the ruler over the kings of the earth. To Him who loved us and washed us from our sins in His own blood, and has made us kings and priests to His God and Father, to Him be glory and dominion forever and ever. Amen (Revelation 1:4-6).

*The grace of our Lord Jesus Christ be with you all. **Amen*** (Revelation 22:21).

- AMEN was at the <u>beginning</u> of the world and will be at the <u>end</u>.
- The world began with AMEN and will finish with AMEN. He is the Beginning and the End.
- The Bible ends with an affirmation that it is "the truth," the hope of glory.

Recommendation and Warnings
1. He knows what you have done; He knows that you are neither cold nor hot. How He wishes (His hope) that you are either one or the other! But because you are lukewarm, neither hot nor cold, He will spit you out of His mouth! (Revelation 3:15-16).
   - Being a lukewarm Christian is being a hypocrite, which is very dangerous because you are neither here nor there. Deceptive is the word for lukewarm Christians.
   - You are not certain where you stand and what you stand for. You are lost between two faiths— knowing "the truth" and not knowing "the truth."
   - You are the one who persecuted Christ on the cross. He would rather have you with Him because not being with Him tells Him how distant and

lost you are from Him, and how capable He is of restoring you into His kingdom. It gives Him the opportunity to show you His love and gives Him an idea of who you are.

- The people God allows into His kingdom are those who give up their self-righteousness and take up His cross. He will be your Savior and open the door of salvation to you.

- You are the reason for His Second Coming, to give you enough time to surrender to the cross. You have the chance to change for the banquet.

So the servants went out into the streets and gathered all the people they could find, good and bad alike; and the wedding hall was filled with people (Matthew 22:10).

Chapter Nine

Neither Hot nor Cold

The king went in to look at the guests and saw a man who was not wearing wedding clothes. Friend, how did you get in here without wedding clothes, the king asked him? But the man said nothing. Then the king told the servants, tie him up hand and foot, and throw him outside in the dark. There he will cry and gnash his teeth. And Jesus concluded, many are invited, but few are chosen (Matthew 22:11-14).

As the King, He will take a look at the guests in the feast room, and He will find a man who has not been invited to the feast—a party gate crasher.

- How will He find out that the man has not been invited?
- What will betray him?

His actions would betray him, and he would be wearing the wrong clothes for the feast—the clothes of deception. He has not changed into the right clothing—the garment of righteousness, which is achieved by going to the cross of salvation. Without salvation:

- Our lives would be cut short by our sins.
- Our garment would be soiled with sin.
- Our invitation would be scrapped.
- You would not make it to the feast.

This man lacked the garment of righteousness, and he thought he could make it to the feast through bypassing the feet of the cross, the same place where you ought to give up your will and pick up the will of God. He will bypass the elements of salvation and cheat his way out and make it to the feast without going through the cross. His mistake would be taking the things of God for granted and making it to the feast without accepting the invitation.

A lukewarm Christian thinks he or she is okay as long as they remain as they are in their Christian lives and make no way to the cross for their daily bread. He leads a self-righteous life and deceives everyone about who he really is by trying to imitate God in everything he does. He is living a sinful life without Christ. He is living his life outside the law and does not attempt to change it.

The Lukewarm and the Cold

The lukewarm Christian is worse than the cold Christian because he knows the truth, but he chooses not to abide by it. The cold Christian, like Pilate, knows not the truth, so he has been given a chance to know the truth. Coming to know the truth offers the opportunity to change. You know not the law, but you are prepared to change your concept of the law to the truth. Unlike the lukewarm Christian who knows the truth, you have the truth available to you, but you choose not to abide by it. You do nothing with the truth and leave it idle to die in you; you render it useless.

You are the laborer in the field, yielding nothing to the seed that has been planted in you. You are in the Lord's field, cultivating His land, but you are yielding nothing because you have sold your soul to the Enemy!

The Enemy is yielding fruit for his kingdom of darkness through you. Be careful, therefore, of what you do and with whom you associate. There are enemies out there recruiting for the kingdom of darkness. You will lose your place in the kingdom of God to someone acceptable. The cold Christian is prepared to forfeit his self-desire for the kingdom of God. You are yielding nothing for the kingdom of God as opposed to the cold Christian who knows nothing. Your place in the kingdom of God will be given to the cold Christian.

Some of you have heard the Gospel of Christ and still lead a sinful life. You are self-righteous, but as you get to know Jesus Christ, you will become Christ-centered. You will move by the Spirit of God and become righteous in His name.

You say, "I am rich and well off; I have all that I need." But you do not know how miserable and pitiful you are! You are poor, naked, and blind. The Lord then advises you as follows:

a) Buy pure gold from Him in order to be rich.
b) Buy white clothing to dress and cover up your shameful nakedness.
c) Buy some ointment to put on your eyes so that you may see (Revelation 3:17-18).

You say, "I am rich and well off…"

If you are rich and well off as you say you are, then buy yourself the cloth of righteousness because you will need the righteousness of God to enter the Lord's gate when He comes. You cannot enter His gates anyhow—no matter which of the twelve entrances to the New Jerusalem you try to use; it must come with sacrifice. All those who live according to the Word of God, live by His principles. All those entrances come with dedication and devotion.

To share in the righteousness of God, you have to be humble, poor in spirit, and dedicated to the Lord. The Lord's salvation is not lightly taken; it needs dedication and surrendering your will to Him. In another sense, the rich cannot purchase Christ's righteousness because you cannot dedicate yourself to Him since you have everything you need at your disposal and lack nothing to render yourself to make Him your God. However, a man with a pure heart will dedicate to Him regardless of his position—rich or poor. If you say I am rich (worldly) and well off; I have all I need, well, all these luxuries are short-lived.

You cannot be a slave of two masters; you will hate one and love the other; you will be loyal to one and despise the other. You cannot serve both God and money.

This is why I tell you: do not be worried about the food and drink you need in order to stay alive, or about clothes for your body. After all, isn't life worth more than food? And isn't the body worth more than clothes? Look at the birds: they do not plant seeds, gather a harvest and put it in barns; yet your Father in heaven takes care of them! Aren't you worth much more than birds? Can any of you live a bit longer by worrying about it?

And why worry about clothes? Look how the wild flowers grow: they do not work or make clothes for themselves. But I tell you that not even King Solomon with all his wealth had clothes as beautiful as one of these flowers. It is God who clothes the wild grass—grass that is here today and gone tomorrow, burned up in the oven. Won't he be all the more sure to clothe you? What little faith you have! So do not start worrying: Where will my food come from? or my drink? or my clothes? (These are the things the pagans are always concerned about.) Your Father in heaven knows that you need all these things. Instead, be concerned above everything else with the Kingdom of God and with what he requires of you, and he will provide you with all these other things (Matthew 6:24-33).

The love of money is the root of all evil!

Well, religion does make us very rich, if we are satisfied with what we have. What did we bring into the world? Nothing! What can we take out of the world? Nothing! So then, if we have food and clothes that should be enough for us. But those who want to get rich fall into temptation and are caught in the trap of many foolish and harmful desires, which pull them down to ruin and destruction. For the love of money is a source of all kinds of evil. Some have been so eager to have it that they have wandered away from the faith and have broken their hearts with many sorrows (I Timothy 6:6-10).

Thieves will steal and moths will destroy your worldly wealth.

Do not store up riches for yourselves here on earth, where moths and rust destroy, and robbers break in and steal. Instead, store up riches for yourselves in heaven, where moths and rust cannot destroy, and robbers cannot break in and steal. For your heart will always be where your riches are (Matthew 6:19-21).

If your riches are in heaven, your heart will always be in God's kingdom where all of your riches are—not worldly riches. It is your inheritance for being the child of God.

You are *poor*, *naked*, and *blind* like a bat that cannot see where it's going.

God stripped off His glory from man at the time man sinned against Him in the Garden of Eden, but God has made a provision for you to regain His glory through a sacrifice. You will have to sacrifice yourself to Him in order to regain your glory. You will be clothed again with His glory with the condition that you will serve Him alone. You were once richly clothed and could see, but now you are poor, naked, and blind because of your sin.

The Lord's glory was taken away from you; now you can see your nakedness through the blemished clothes you are wearing. You are rich but not for long. Yours will be the story of the rich man and Lazarus in Luke 16:19-32. The rich man exchanged his worldly riches for poverty in hell. He did not lack anything on earth, but he lacked prosperity in the kingdom of God. He did not have what it takes to make it to God's kingdom, depending upon everything he had. He lacked riches in heaven and had no inheritance there for himself. Earthly things will pass away one day; they are short-lived, but the things of God are eternal and will render you prosperous in His kingdom.

Prosperity is not the key to God's kingdom, regardless of how much you have; rather, **simplicity** is the key. The simple-minded person has access to the Lord's feast due to their humility. The poor in spirit also exchanges his poverty for the riches in heaven. **Humility** is the keyword for the unrighteous man to embrace in order to enter into God's kingdom.

Jesus said to him, if you want to be perfect, go and sell all you have and give the money to the poor, and you will have riches in heaven; then come and follow me. When the young man heard this, he went away sad, because he was very rich. Jesus then said to his disciples, I assure you: it will be very hard for rich people to enter the Kingdom of heaven. I repeat: it is much harder for a rich person to enter the Kingdom of God than for a camel to go through the eye of a needle (Matthew 19:21-24).

The Parable of the Rich Fool
A man in the crowd said to Jesus, Teacher, tell my brother to divide with me the property our father left us. Jesus

answered him, friend, who gave me the right to judge or to divide the property between you two? And he went on to say to them all, **watch out and guard yourselves from every kind of greed; because your true life is not made up of the things you own, no matter how rich you may be.** *Then Jesus told them this parable:*

There was once a rich man who had land which bore good crops. He began to think to himself, I don't have a place to keep all my crops. What can I do? This is what I will do, he told himself; I will tear down my barns and build bigger ones, where I will store the grain and all my other goods. Then I will say to myself, Lucky man! You have all the good things you need for many years. Take life easy, eat, drink, and enjoy yourself but God said to him, you fool! This very night you will have to give up your life; then who will get all these things you have kept for yourself? **And Jesus concluded, this is how it is with those who pile up riches for themselves but are not rich in God's sight** (Luke 12:12-21).

Life is much more important than food, and the body much more important than clothes (Luke 12:23).

Instead, be concerned with his Kingdom, and he will provide you with these things (Luke 12:31).

You Are Poor

Six days before the Passover, Jesus went to Bethany, the home of Lazarus, the man he had raised from death. They prepared a dinner for him there, which Martha helped serve; Lazarus was one of those who were sitting at the table with Jesus. Then Mary took a whole pint of a very expensive perfume made of pure nard, poured it on Jesus' feet, and wiped them with her hair. The sweet smell of the perfume filled the whole house (John 12:1-3).

Although you are rich in your eyes, in the sight of God, you are poor. You have gained worldly wealth but no eternal wealth; you are poor in His kingdom. But pour your "riches" on Him who created you, and He will place you in His kingdom. He will honor your dedication and make you the king that He wants you to be. Sacrifice your life to Him, and you will have no regrets. Share your destiny with Him, and you will see what He will make of you. Destiny is your life and how you lead it is up to you, but God is the master of your destiny; He is prepared to change your destiny round and make you rich in His kingdom. Your destiny is in your hand, you can either make or break it. Change your mind and follow Jesus Christ.

(Read Isaiah 55:1-2; Matthew 13:44; 1 Peter 1:7.)

Buy gold from me, a pure gold in order to be rich…

The Faithful Church is made of beaten pure gold. The Church is enriched with pure gold throughout. You will never lack anything in that kingdom because God has designed it to supply you with all His riches. He has made it of pure gold (Revelation 21:15-21). God makes the best gold—the purest ever through His furnace of fire. He burns out every impurity and creates gold that is unblemished and worth thousands of praises. He makes it impeccably strong and inaccessible to people. In this case, I am referring to purity, divinity, and the scarcity of His gold. He makes it to suit you and your appearance. How do you buy into the righteousness of Christ?

You are naked.
The word "*naked*" has the following meanings:
- "Having the body completely unclothed"
- "Having <u>no covering</u>; bare; <u>exposed</u>"
- "With no qualification or concealment"
- "With no defense, protection, or shield"
- "Defenseless, unclothed, unprotected, unassisted, bare, exposed, helpless, vulnerable, unarmed"

Revelation 19:5-8 (emphasis added)
Then there came from the throne the sound of a voice, saying, Praise our God, all his servants and all people, both great and small, who have reverence for him! Then I heard what sounded like a crowd, like the sound of a roaring waterfall, like loud peals of thunder.

> *I heard them say, Praise God! For the Lord, our Almighty God, is King! Let us rejoice and be glad; let us praise his greatness! For the time has come for the wedding of the Lamb, and his bride has prepared herself for it. She has been given **clean shining linen** to wear. (The linen is the good deeds of God's people.)*

Buy also white clothing to dress yourself and cover up your shameful nakedness.

The clean, shining linen of the white garment symbolizes *righteousness*, the Lord's Holiness covering your spiritual nakedness (your self-righteousness). You will share in His righteousness. *How do you buy into the righteousness of God?*

You are blind.

You are spiritually blind to the things of God. You see what you see, but you do not understand what you see because you need spiritual eyes to be able to see beyond what you see in the natural. You can see, but you are blind to God's Word. You cannot perceive His things because you are blind to the truth.

The word *blind* has the following meanings:
- "Sightless, render unable to see"
- "Unable or unwilling to perceive or understand"
- "Lacking reason or purpose"
- "Difficult to comprehend or see; illegible"
- "To deprive of perception or insight"

Similar words to *blind* include the following: sightless, unaware of, deaf to, ignorant of, heedless of, unmindful of, unquestioning, unreasoning, mindless, intimidate, confuse.

But it was to us that God made known his secret by means of his Spirit. The Spirit searches everything, even the hidden depths of God's purposes. It is only our own spirit within us that knows all about us; in the same way, only God's Spirit knows all about God (1 Corinthians 2:10-11).

Buy also some ointment to put on your eyes, so that you may see.

This is the ointment that the Lord makes with His saliva and dust from the ground (earth) to save our vision about who He is in entirety (See John 9:1-11).

He came to earth to save us from the darkness. He created man to be in the dark of things. He removed the knowledge of good and bad from man until the appointed time, but the Devil came and gave you his version of the knowledge of what is good and bad. The Devil persuaded man to follow him into his world of devious activities, but God sent His Son to elevate man from that darkness, opening his eyes to the light—His true version of the knowledge of what is good and what is bad. Jesus opened man's eyes to the truth.

- He is the light of your salvation.
- He is the Sovereign God.

- He is the Almighty God.
- The One who speaks and it is done.

Thank You, God, for Your love in our lives!

Chapter Ten

The Blind Man

As Jesus was walking along, he saw a man who had been born blind. His disciples asked him, "Teacher, whose sin caused him to be born blind? Was it his own or his parents' sin?" Jesus answered, "His blindness has nothing to do with his sins or his parents' sins. He is blind so that God's power might be seen at work in him. As long as it is day, we must do the work of him who sent me; night is coming when no one can work. While I am in the world, I am the light for the world." After he said this, Jesus spat on the ground and made some mud with the spittle; he rubbed the mud on the man's eyes and told him, "Go and wash your face in the Pool of Siloam." (This name means "Sent.") So the man went, washed his face, and came back seeing. His neighbours, then, and the people who had seen him begging before this, asked, "Isn't this the man who used to sit and beg?" Some said, "He is the one," but others said, "No he isn't; he just looks like him." So the man himself said, "I am the man." "How is it that you can now see?" they asked him. He answered, "The man called Jesus made some mud, rubbed it on my eyes, and told me to go to Siloam and wash my face. So I went, and as soon as I washed, I could see" (John 9:1-11).

Healing the Blind Man

Points to Consider:

1) The blind man and his blindness
- Was he born blind? (v. 1).
- Whose sin caused his blindness? (Vv. 2-3).
- His birth
- His begging

2) Jesus, and his healing
- His mission
- His method of healing
- The significance of the instructions given

3) After the healing
- His conception of Jesus

- Before personally setting eyes on Him
- After setting eyes on Him

Jesus' disciples did not understand the significance of what Jesus has done and interpreted the man's blindness as a curse. Their response was disregarding the works of the Lord that caused the man's blindness before he was born. We are always judged before we prove our innocence. The disciples did not know the cause of the man's blindness, but they had already judged him. This is today's Church: judging people before getting to know them (Read Luke 5).

The Blind Man

Was he born blind?

Naturally, man is spiritually born blind to the things and nature of God. The Lord did not reveal everything about His kingdom upon creation. He hid certain things about Himself from us; therefore, the reason He calls us His earthly treasures. He has hidden treasures in His Book and reveals them to those who love and seek Him.

If you do not love Jesus, you do not get to see the mind of God. God calls them treasures in His Word—secrets revealed upon acceptance. You might be in the house of the Lord, but revelation will not be accessed unless you have an established covenant with Him. He made us blind to some of His things for His glory to be manifested at the right time. He made us blind for a reason and a season, but the Devil turned it around. He kept you in the dark about the key to the tree that holds the knowledge of what is good and bad (Genesis 5:15-17).

In Genesis 3:1-7, the Devil comes with his devious ways to man to share his counterfeit version of the knowledge of what is good and bad. He persuades man into his world of devious activities, but the Lord offers man a redemption path (Genesis 3:21). He has made clothes from animal skins with which to clothe you. He has made a provision to recover you from your sin. God has sent His Son to open our eyes to the truth—the true version of the knowledge of what is good and bad.

Whose sin caused his blindness?

His disciples asked him, "Teacher, whose sin caused him to be born blind? Was it his own or his parents' sin?" Jesus answered, "His blindness has nothing to do with his sins or his parents' sins. He is blind so that God's power might be seen at work in him" (John 9:2-3).

The disciples wanted to know if the man was born blind because of the sin of his parents [referring to Adam and Eve], which has been carried on to generations. Jesus answered, "No. This is the work of God in order to glorify His name when the time comes." He created man in that same manner for a reason. He specifically created man blind to His things for a specific purpose and time. He has done that for His kingdom to flourish without the help of judging the truth. God created man that way before sin entered the world. He made man spiritually blind to His things until the exact time that He has purposed to unveil the truth to you.

His birth

In Genesis 2:7, in the Garden of Eden, God took soil from the ground—the womb of the earth—and formed man out of it. The blind man was formed from clay (soil + water). The Garden of Eden was the birthplace of man. Upon man's blindness, he lacked nothing in the Garden. God provided man with everything he needed.

The first Adam, made of earth, came from the earth; the second Adam came from heaven. Those who belong to the earth are like the one who was made of earth; those who are of heaven are like the one who came from heaven. Just as we wear the likeness of the man-made of earth, so we will wear the likeness of the Man from heaven (1 Corinthians 15:47-49).

His begging

The phrase *to beg* has the following meanings:
- To ask someone for money, food, and so on.
- Ask to obtain free.

When God created man, He provided everything necessary that man would need to live in the Garden of Eden (Genesis 2:8-17).

Man lacked nothing in the Garden and have everything needed for our survival at our disposal. Knowing your blindness to His things, God still provided what you needed to grow in His kingdom until the Devil came to take all that away from you. The Devil is still going to and fro, looking for someone to devour.

After the Fall, God sent man out of the Garden, and he lost all the provisions that God had lovingly provided for him (Genesis 3:22-24).

With the curse of our disobedience, the covenant formed with Satan and our blindness to the things of God proved difficult for man. Man had to beg for alms in the hands of the Devil for survival. You seek alms from all sorts of people for survival, and due to your blindness, you do not know who these people really are in the spirit. You obtain alms from people you should not have. The man that God created is begging for alms. Man was not created to beg, but to be fruitful. What turned man into a beggar? Man had it upon his blindness, and now he is begging for alms. You are blind to the truth of God's Word and the one the Devil told you was a counterfeit and twisted truth. Spiritually, this means that you have been seeking help from other sources (gods) for survival—worshiping and servicing other gods.

(Read Isaiah 5:13; Jeremiah 5:4; Ezekiel 44:23)

My people <u>are doomed</u> because they <u>do not acknowledge</u> me. You priests have refused to acknowledge me and have rejected my teaching, and so I reject you and will not acknowledge your sons as my priests (Hosea 4:6 Emphasis Added).

My people <u>are destroyed</u> for <u>lack of knowledge</u>. Because you have rejected knowledge, I also will reject you from being priest for Me; because you have forgotten the law of your God, I also will forget your children (Hosea 4:6; NKJV).

Jesus and His Healing

His Mission

As long as it is day, we must do the work of him who sent me; night is coming when no one can work. While I am in the world, I am the light for the world (John 9:4-5).

A time will come when you cannot work in His fields. A time will come when man cannot go to the cross for salvation. As long as that time has not come, open your heart to His Word. You must keep on cultivating His land and yield more fruits for His kingdom until He comes—the *end time*. You must utilize the time that you have now!

You are like light for the whole world. A city built on a hill cannot be hid. No one lights a lamp and puts it under a bowl; instead it is put on the lampstand, where it gives light for everyone in the house. In the same way your light must shine before people, so that they will see the good things you do and praise your Father in Heaven (Matthew 5:14-16).

God sent His only begotten Son to elevate you from darkness and open your eyes to the light—God's true version of the knowledge of what is good and bad.

Jesus spoke to the Pharisees again. I am the light of the world, he said. Whoever follows me will have the light of life and will never walk in darkness (John 8:12).

His Method of Healing

After he said this, Jesus spat on the ground and made some mud with the spittle; he rubbed the mud on the man's eyes and told him, "Go and wash your face in the Pool of Siloam." (This name means "Sent.") So the man went, washed his face, and came back seeing (John 9:6-7).

After Jesus said "I am the light of the world," He started healing the blind man. Notice that Jesus did not ask the blind man to be healed of his blindness. He did not ask him whether or not he wanted to be healed. This was not a question of faith or belief; it was a question of purpose. Jesus needed not to ask the blind man as He had said in the previous verse. The blindness was purposely caused by His Father so that His power might be seen at work in him.

For this reason, God sent Jesus into the world—to save the dying world of its blindness. God has already instructed Him to execute that mission, so He needs no affirmation from the blind man to be healed. He proved both His submission and authority to God. He is obeying His Father's instruction to do what He has asked Him to do, whether or not the blind man likes it.

> *Everyone whom my Father gives me will come to me. I will never turn away anyone who comes to me, because I have come down from heaven to do not my own will but the will of him who sent me. And it is the will of him who sent me that I should not lose any of all those he has given me, but that I should raise them all to life on the last day. For what my Father wants is that all who see the Son and believe in him should have eternal life. And I will raise them to life on the last day* (John 6:37-40).

He did that to open our spiritual eyes to the truth; the things of God, from which we are blinded in the beginning.

1. Jesus does not need his faith first to heal him.
2. He has been ushered into the world to proclaim the message of the kingdom to the blind and point out the right path to salvation.

First, Jesus spat in the soil—the ground of the earth from which man was created (a mixture of spittle {saliva} and soil).

• Why the mixture of spittle and soil?

(Read John 7:37-39; Leviticus 23:36; Ezekiel 47:1; Zechariah 14:8; 1 Corinthians 15:45).

Then the L*ORD* *God took some soil from the ground and formed a man out of it; he breathed life-giving breath into his nostrils and the man began to live* (Genesis 2:7).

For the scripture says, the first man, Adam, was created a living being; but the last Adam is the life-giving Spirit (1 Corinthians 15:45).

Man was formed at the beginning of creation from mud (soil + water) and the life-giving breath of God. You are made from the soil of the earth, as such, your healing process will involve the soil (dust) from which you were created and the life-giving Spirit that breathed into your nostrils. These are the initial ingredients for our creation.

Jesus created clay, which represents who you are in the Lord, a creature of mud (soil + water). Through saliva, a person's DNA can be determined by testing and the DNA of Jesus Christ is the life-giving Spirit which was breathed into man at creation. He has the non-contaminated life-giving breath in Him due to the circumstances around His birth, and this will change your situation. God mixed the two components (His righteousness and your flesh), rubbed it on the blind man's eyes and came out with a victorious result.

Second, He placed the clay on the man's eyes to illustrate His resurrection from the dark.

He placed it on the eyes, which is the gateway to his soul and planted in him the healing power. He resurrected the blind man from the dark and made him aware of his surroundings through his soul. The life-giving Spirit (spittle) immortalizes his body, and therefore, makes him aware of his surroundings. The soul is the driving seat of man, and the healing of your soul heals the whole being.

Third, Jesus then said to the man, *"Go and wash your face in the Pool of Siloam (Sent)."* He said to the man, "Go to the 'Sent' to wash your soul to get healed." He pointed to him the right place to go for healing. He ordered him to go and wash his face in the Pool of Siloam. Literally, Jesus is saying, "I have resurrected you from the dark and have immortalized your body. Now, go to the brazen laver—*the Word of God; Sent; Jesus*—to wash your soul with the Word of God—the truth that has been shown to you."

The brazen laver where the healing word would cleanse and heal your soul and the washing of the mud are the antidotes to your physical problem (disability). But the spiritual meaning of the washing is to bring you out of the darkness into light. For this reason, the first thing he saw after washing his face was light, which stands for "truth"—the Word of God, which is Jesus Christ. The man saw the light through his soul (eyes).

The washing of the clay opened his eyes to the truth—the light. He has been saved from darkness into light.

Fourth, the man went, washed his face, and came back with his sight restored. He did not ask anyone to help him to the pool because salvation is a one-man job, and no one does it for you. You must realize that you need salvation, and you alone must make your way to the cross for salvation. Since no one can do it for you, you have to take the necessary steps; He will direct your path. The Pool of Siloam is, in that sense, the cross on Calvary.

- How did the man find his way to the pool unaided?

He was led to the pool by the life-saving Spirit planted in him. When the Word of God hits you, it immortalizes your body. You know where you are going through discernment; even though you cannot see, the knowledge makes you see. He went, washed his soul, and got healed.

- For how long did he wash his face?

The Bible does not shed light on that aspect, but we do know he was healed in the end.

He came to understand the things of God and moved toward restoration. You learn the things about His kingdom through the washing of face in the brazen laver. It reflects your soul and you'll begin to see things clearer as you wash along.

Once he got healed, he decided to take up the cross and follow Jesus.

After the Healing

His conception of Jesus

> *His neighbours, then, and the people who had seen him begging before this, asked, "Isn't this the man who used to sit and beg?" Some said, "He is the one," but others said, "No he isn't; he just looks like him." So the man himself said, "I am the man"* (John 9:8-9).

Once your sight is restored and when you come face to face with *the truth*, your life takes a turn for the best, and people tend not to recognize you for who you are now.

> *Anyone who is joined to Christ is a new being; the old is gone, the new has come* (2 Corinthians 5:17).

Everything about you—your personality, perspective, knowledge, etc., changes for the best. You have become aware of your surroundings and need no alms from strangers. Your appearance has changed.

> *He answered, "The man called Jesus made some mud, rubbed it on my eyes, and told me to go to Siloam and wash my face. So I went, and as soon as I washed, I could see." They said to him, "Where is he?" He said, "I don't know"* (John 9:11-12).

In this passage, he has not really come to know Jesus in the physical sense, but spiritually. When Jesus rubbed the healing balm on his eyes, he was blind at the time and did not actually see Him after being healed. For him to really know Jesus, he had to take up the cross and have an intimate relationship with Him. This is only done by carrying His cross as he did.

Before Setting His Eyes on the Healer

Then they took to the Pharisees the man who had been blind. The day that Jesus made the mud and cured him of his blindness was a Sabbath. The Pharisees, then, asked the man again how he had received his sight. He told them, "He put some mud on my eyes; I washed my face, and now I can see."

Some of the Pharisees said, "The man who did this cannot be from God, for he does not obey the Sabbath law."

Others, however, said, "How could a man who is a sinner perform such miracles as these?" And there was a division among them.

So the Pharisees asked the man once more, "You say he cured you of your blindness—well, what do you say about him?"

"He is a prophet," the man answered.

The Jewish authorities, however, were not willing to believe that he had been blind and could now see, until they called his parents and asked them, "Is this your son? You say that he was born blind; how is it, then, that he can now see?"

His parents answered, "We know that he is our son, and we know that he was born blind. But we do not know how it is that he is now able to see, nor do we know who cured him of his blindness. Ask him; he is old enough, and he can answer for himself!" His parents said this because they were afraid of the Jewish authorities, who had already agreed that anyone who said he believed that Jesus was the Messiah would be expelled from the synagogue. That is why his parents said, "He is old enough; ask him!"

A second time they called back the man who had been born blind, and said to him, "Promise before God that you will tell the truth! We know that this man who cured you is a sinner."

"I do not know if he is a sinner or not," the man replied. "One thing I do know: I was blind, and now I see."

"What did he do to you?" they asked. "How did he cure you of your blindness?"

"I have already told you," he answered, "and you would not listen. Why do you want to hear it again? Maybe you, too, would like to be his disciples?"

They insulted him and said, "You are that fellow's disciple; but we are Moses' disciples. We know that God spoke to Moses; as for that fellow, however, we do not even know where he comes from!"

The man answered, "What a strange thing that is! You do not know where he comes from, but he cured me of my blindness! We know that God does not listen to sinners; he does listen to people who respect him and do what he wants them to do. Since the beginning of the world nobody has ever heard of anyone giving sight to a person born blind. Unless this man came from God, he would not be able to do a thing."

They answered, "You were born and brought up in sin—and you are trying to teach us?" And they expelled him from the synagogue (John 9:13-34).

Because the man hadn't enjoyed an intimate fellowship with Jesus, his only picture of Him was a man who had rubbed mud on his eyes and healed him of his blindness. He directed him to where to get his healing, and that is what he did and that is all he knew about Him. The formerly blind man could not really tell who Jesus was. Since his judgment of who Jesus is was not certain, he claimed Jesus as a prophet and then a man of God. Because unless He came from God, He would not be able to teach him all these things to do.

After setting eyes on Jesus
Spiritual Blindness

When Jesus heard what had happened, he found the man and asked him, "Do you believe in the Son of Man?" The man answered, "Tell me who he is, sir, so that I can believe in him!" Jesus said to him, "You have already seen him, and he is the one who is talking with you now." "I believe, Lord!" the man said, and knelt down before Jesus. Jesus said, "I came to this world to judge, so that the blind should see and those who see should become blind." Some Pharisees who were there with him heard him say this and asked him, "Surely you don't mean that we are blind, too?" Jesus answered, "If you were blind, then you would not be guilty; but since you claim that you can see, this means that you are still guilty" (John 9:35-41).

When the man came face to face with Jesus through intimate worship, Jesus revealed Himself to him and showed him many things about God's kingdom. You can only know the truth by having an intimate relationship with Jesus, the Son of God. Jesus asked him, *"Do you believe in the Son of Man? The man answered, "Tell me who he is, Sir, so that I can believe in him!"*

This man wanted to know the truth, and Jesus told him he had already seen *the truth* because He was the truth. *"I believe, Lord!"* he responded. (This time, he did not say "Sir!" because he had seen the revelation of the truth, and he bowed down before "the Truth" and worshipped Him).

Jesus said, I came to this world to judge, so that the blind should see and those who see should become blind (John 9:38).

How Can You Buy All these Things (Gold, White Garment, and Eye Ointment) from the Son of God?

These three elements of salvation can be obtained by surrendering to Jesus and selling all your earthly riches for His poverty. You have to sell all your earthly riches to come to Him. All these things are sold at the feet of the cross by burning off every sacrifice on the brazen altar to make it to salvation. Burning off the sacrifice is the selling of your worldly riches for poverty to ascertain riches in God's kingdom.

Salvation is a long process, and time is needed to consume all your riches. The brazen altar will burn out all of your worldly attitudes such as pride, arrogance, greed, and so on. You have to give up everything: all of your worldly wealth—*wrong attitudes, your unrighteousness* for His cross and for salvation to come to you. Salvation is the sign needed to create eternal life.

(Read Luke 18:18-30; Matthew 19:16-30; Mark 10:17-31).

Eternal life ≡ True life
To receive eternal life (true life):
- You **must** sacrifice yourself on the altar. Until you give up your will, which belongs to the world, go back to

the world of the poor and pick up God's will, which entitles you to riches in heaven, you will not have eternal life after this world.

- Drop off your will, pick up the Father's will, and follow Jesus!

You exchange your poverty for God's riches in Heaven. The only way the rich can do that is by giving up their worldly wealth like Jesus did by taking off His royal robe and tying the towel of servanthood around His waist to serve the disciples. He became poor for your sake.

In Matthew 19:16-24, the rich man became very sad because of his possessions. He is really rich and cannot afford to give up his luxury possessions and all that comes with it. You cannot be a slave to two masters. Drop off your pride (self-will) for humility (God's will)!

And everyone who has left houses or brothers or sisters or father or mother or children or fields for my sake, will receive a hundred times more and will be given eternal life (Matthew 19:29).

Summary

Watchful Servants (Luke 12:35-40)

The final message was sent out when God came to us in the form of man, Immanuel (His Son, Jesus Christ). He gave you the last invitation into God's kingdom to join the feast.

Verse 40, which says, *Jesus answered, "I tell you that if they keep quiet, the stones themselves will start shouting"* is the calling of the people on the street to join the feast because of your refusal to the invitation (See Luke 19:37-40).

Jerusalem rejoices because of what the Lord *has done. She is like a bride dressed for her wedding. God has clothed her with salvation and victory* (Isaiah 61:10).

He has covered you with the white garment—the robe of righteousness. The message is sent to all corners of the world—*during the feeding of the 4000*—making haste of time, of how near the coming of God's kingdom is. It portrays the picture of the coming of God's kingdom and alerts you to sacrifice your will and turn away from your sin. The message has gone worldwide to sinners and to the churches which are supposed to be worshipping God. It warns the churches to turn away from their sins. You are the people who qualify for the feast, but your behavior and style of living condemn you from inheriting His kingdom. Therefore, God sent His Son to warn us to turn away from our sins, i.e., *wash your clothes clean.*

His Son specifically addressed who He was to you, your sins, your strong points, what He will do to help you recover your blessings if you succeed individually. You refused Him entirely to turn away from your sins, although you claim to be a child of God. How can you be a child of God if you do not listen to your Father? You lead your life as a prostitute (meaning: *a person considered as having compromised principles for personal gain*) and full of incarnations. You do not believe in Jesus (*hypocrite*) and have made your own incarnations of Him, which has brought the wrath between you and God.

Our behavior is appalling and has caused God to make another announcement to invite anyone—good or bad—outside the church to the feast, provided they will take up the cross and follow His Son, Jesus Christ, i.e., *put on the appropriate clothes.*

Taking up the cross and needing salvation are the proper garments for entry to the banquet.

Part Five

The Principles

True Happiness
"Happy are those who know they are spiritually poor;
the Kingdom of heaven belongs to them!
"Happy are those who mourn;
God will comfort them!
"Happy are those who are humble;
they will receive what God has promised!
"Happy are those whose greatest desire is to do
what God requires;
God will satisfy them fully!
"Happy are those who are merciful to others;

God will be merciful to them!
"Happy are the pure in heart;
they will see God!
"Happy are those who work for peace;
God will call them his children!
"Happy are those who are persecuted because they do
what God requires;
the Kingdom of heaven belongs to them!
"Happy are you when people insult you and persecute
you and tell all kinds of evil lies against you because you
are my followers. Be happy and glad, for a great reward
is kept for you in heaven. This is how the prophets who
lived before you were persecuted.
- Matthew 5:3-12

Chapter Eleven

Of the Church

The purpose of this book series is to bring God's people into a state of togetherness in the Church. We are apart from each other due to our differences in beliefs. God has made Himself clear about diversity in Paul's writings. We are to reconcile with anyone we hate or with whom we have a grudge for any other reason. As the Lord pours His anointing on the earth, He will declare His ways to us.

The Devil has his way of making life difficult for people. He tampers with everything: trust, lives, freedom, necessities, and surety. The Devil is always doing something that brings unhappiness in life, including causing diversity. He creates his own atmosphere, orchestrating diverse ways to follow in order to capture us in our tracks.

Difficult it is, but God has given us the power (ability) to overcome the tricks of the Enemy. The Devil is and has always been a liar. Men who live by God's principles do not allow the Devil to wreck their lives.

Let your light shine in darkness so that everyone who sees you will know where you are coming from. Light shines in total darkness.

The Principles

The principles of man are delicate in their own way, considering how man allows change into his life without reason. Magnify the Lord with all your heart!

The noun *principle* has the following meanings:

- "A truth or general law that is used as a basis for a theory or system of belief."
- "Rules or beliefs governing the way you behave"

The adjective *omnipotent* has the following meanings:

- "Infinite in power, as God"
- "Having very great or unlimited authority or power"
- The omnipotent God is all of the following:
- Oneness
- Totality
- The God of wonders
- The everlasting God
- The I Am that I Am

- The One who never lies in our midst
- The God of gods
- The sovereign Lord
- The Master of all creation
- The One who says "yes" and abides with it
- The Leader of the world
- The Most High God

Nothing is bigger than God—especially our worries and troubles!

The "Sermon on the Mount" (Matthew 5:3-12; Luke 6:20-23) is the "principle of the Church." This passage reveals the showing of love, the return of love, the merciful, the adoration, the faithfulness, the humbleness, the deceived, the emotionally wrecked, and the elect. The principles are simple for anyone to follow, which is how we should be leading our life in Christ. This is the Church in us because we are one in Christ. He is the God for all mankind; He is the Church that lies in us. He is Christ our Lord who lives in us and resurrects us. His principles shall be on our lips day and night, and His kingdom shall be our kingdom in the Lord.

When God shines His light on His Word, His principles become easy to understand by man. A measure of faith is when our faith is measured with the love of God, when we lead a good and faithful life. That faith (Revelation 12:15) is measured with the rod in His hands!

- *How do you assess yourself in the environment of the Church?*
- *Do you assess it by using God's principles to measure your faith in the Church?*

These principles should rule our church and guide our life. Rewriting the principles will be the forbidden fruit in the Garden of Eden that is untouchable and unamendable. You should not touch the fruit of the tree which God has planted in the middle of the Garden. This fruit was eaten by Adam and Eve, the first sinners of this world. Through that tree, God's salvation will come to man in the end.

The story of the Garden of Eden is what we are about to experience in this world. The Garden is where man's freedom was exchanged for that of the serpent. The story of the Garden is to prepare us beforehand of what is about to happen in the world that we're creating by our own will. So, the story of the Garden of Eden has not yet happened; it is yet to happen to us. It is the world where the Enemy will persuade man to go against the will of God.

We learned that story in the Old Testament. The forbidden fruit of the Lord is our independence as children of God, which will be taken from us. We will suffer in the hands of the Enemy, but the Lord will come to our aid to rescue us. The whole meaning of the Garden of Eden is to bring us salvation in the end. The story of the Garden is a prophecy of what is to happen.

Look at what is going on in this world now. Faith will be tested in all mankind, and our righteousness will be dependent on the Savior. The garden is coming to us soon because the world is full of enemies of the truth.

The Lord is coming soon! The sin of the world is about to enter the Church, and man will need to live on the Lord's righteousness to survive these coming days. The Garden of Eden did not actually happen in the beginning of the world but will happen at the end. As the Word says, "The Lord knows the end from the beginning." He brought the End of His Word to the Beginning of His Word.

From the beginning I predicted the outcome; long ago I foretold what would happen. I said that my plans would never fail, that I would do everything I intended to do. I am calling a man to come from the east; he will swoop down like a hawk and accomplish what I have planned.

I have spoken, and it will be done. "Listen to me, you stubborn people who think that victory is far away. I am bringing the day of victory near—it is not far away at all. My triumph will not be delayed. I will save Jerusalem and bring honour to Israel there" (Isaiah 46:10-13).

The Devil, the old serpent, came into the Garden and changed life for man. The serpent managed to convince man to change his attitude toward God in order for man to breach his contract with God. The appointing of man into the Garden in the beginning and the restoration of man into the Garden after man fell was the work of the Holy Spirit who resides in us.

The Devil deceived man into going against God, his Creator. Our vulnerability was shown by how man fell prey to Satan's lie.

The messages of Matthew 5:3-10 contain all of the principles of God from the "poor in spirit" to "those who are persecuted for righteousness' sake." "The Beatitudes," i.e., true happiness, collaborate with the "Ten Commandments" given to us in Exodus 20:3-17. The two passages complement each other and correspond with each other.

These principles are divided into two groups: Lamentations, which teaches about discipleship, and Deuteronomy, which teaches about the descendants of Adam.

Lamentations is about the discipleship of God in the ancient times, constituting the Messiah in His reign and capitalizing on His own reign. These easy-to-read passages constitute the resurrection of Christ in the latter days, making Jesus Christ a prophet in His days and changed Him into shining armor in the days of famine. An army was resurrected on Jesus' behalf and made Him King over all Israel. Jesus Christ became famous and well-known for His work.

The purpose of God's Church is to reunite His people in captivity to one Church. The Church has its flaws in employing someone outside their camp (*the enemy*) to minister to them about socializing and infrastructure. Of great importance is understanding that the Church turned things around and changed their destiny.

The Church is about God, and God is about the Church. Let God handle the things of the Church, and let us handle that which He has left us in our charge. We must change our attitude toward God and sing the songs that He has given us, so that His house will be free from monsters. We must drive them out and let the Church be clean.

Preach the Word to the congregation, and let His Word be heard. God is God, and nothing is greater than Him! He is the Almighty God, the Maker of heaven and earth, for all that is seen and unseen. These are the secrets of His Word that, in the end, the End will justify the Beginning. Justify His song by His Word!

The purpose of this is to change the prospective of the idea of a well-dedicated or organized Church. The Church can never be organized or dedicated in the presence of the Enemy. Dedication is a delicate matter concerning the principles of a church, in that the owner of the Church is madly in love with the principles, and Satan is invalidated about principles. We, as a church, owe much to the boundaries of principles and need a dedicated principled man to rule over us.

Watch out for those who do evil things, those dogs, those who insist on cutting the body. It is we, not they, who have received the true circumcision, for we worship God by means of his Spirit and rejoice in our life in union with Christ Jesus. We do not put any trust in external ceremonies. I could, of course, put my trust in such things. If any of you think you can trust in external ceremonies, I have even more reason to feel that way (Philippians 3:2-4).

The Book of Lamentations is about a man who finds it very difficult to understand the things of God. He illustrated his strength with a woman who has lost all she owned by decisiveness and has thrown all she had to the cats of her life. The woman did not believe in Him in restoring what she owned, but the love of God is so great that He lifted the woman up from her frustrations and brought her out.

- *Who is this woman?*

Deuteronomy chapter 13 also says that the love of God is like a man's planting in the field of "desperation." A seed finds difficulty in growing among enemies, i.e., weeds. The man makes all the efforts, but all ends in vain. Through desperation, God brought the man out.

- *Who can help the man proceed in life?*

The man did not tell him about his curse and let him believe that all is well. In the middle of the transaction, the old man gave man something to drink and found himself in the midst of angels. He proclaimed his victory at that time and left. Little did the man know that the same old enemy that he had left wandering about was the same man who had changed his destiny—the same old enemy. Nothing has changed here! You have given your prosperity to the Enemy again—the same old enemy in a different form. This is the principle of God's Church in relation to your destiny. The devil you try to avoid is the same devil who took your things away from you.

Therefore, principles dictate that you are not to live outside of your boundaries. You should pray for your enemies but keep them outside of the boundaries of your life. Still, I believe we cannot do without some of our enemies. Why? They help us grow. No doubt, many people have come your way and made things worse for you, but the suffering they caused helped you mature in your Christian walk. You are the Lion of Judah.

Principles are principles! Make no haste in changing things between you and the Enemy. Do not allow the Enemy into your space. The Enemy of old is on a rampage or mission to destroy you with his works.

Twelve Entrances

The twelve entrances are God's people in the Church—the tribe of Israel. They stand for God's Church in the end times. They are the blessed TREE of LIFE in the Garden of Eden. They are the resurrected twelve in the temple of God. They are the people God has hoped for in joining His Church in the end times.

God has made the twelve out of the root of David. He has chosen David's household with the key in the end. The twelve represent the entrances to God in His Church. Generally speaking, the entrances are for man to enter into God's Church as they please and would not be subject to any criticism. The twelve entrances are made for the entry of God's children. The entrances are wide open to the court of the tabernacle to let in people of all origins to be sanctified.

The foundation of the court of the tabernacle was based on the epistles of John. The days of Elijah and the pre-Adamic days when all was nothing are mentioned. The day that Adam was created was the pre-disposition of the law and the anointing of the Church. The disposition of the law in the land and the restoration of man in the Garden reflect the toil of their fathers into getting it right for them.

Chapter Twelve

In the Church

Changes in God's Church will come regarding the principles by which people have to abide. People think differently in the Church environment; they have different principles, different times, and different ideas. These principles are as follows:

1. The Principle of Ideology
2. The Principle of Time
3. The Principle of Unity
4. The Principle of Adoration
5. The Principle of Equality
6. The Principle of Nationalism

7. The Principle of Remuneration
8. The Principle of Faith

The Principle of Ideology

The principle of ideology addresses the uniformity of ideas in the Church. These are the principles by which we live and function in our day-to-day life. The multiple meanings of the word *ideology* include the following:

- "A body of ideas that reflects the beliefs and interests of a nation, political system, etc. and underlies political action"
- "The set of beliefs by which a group or society orders reality so as to render it intelligible"
- "Speculation that is imaginary or visionary"
- "The study of the nature and origin of ideas"

Ideology comes from the word "idea," which means "the cognitive reasoning of man in his state (imaginative state)."

I live by principles, which was an idea instilled in me by my father. Some people would believe living by principles is unnecessary. Our God made rules that we anoint ourselves every day before we approach people in order to be a blessing to them and their families. God has given you the right to bless other people in your midst (John 10:13-18).

In theology, the ideas of people are not governed by them but by the Most High God. We are not thinking on our own but by the blessing of our Lord Jesus Christ, who lives in us.

The principles that govern our lives make us who we are. We are endowed to accomplish their works on earth and bring salvation to the earth.

We are of God only. Maximize yourself in teaching others who God is and create a new heart in people.

Ideology is "the principle of managing the works of God, as well as the idea behind church and the idea that made church." The ideology of the principles of the Church is **humility. Humble yourself!**

The Principle of Time

Time is a matter that should be considered in how we live our life. If we add together all those times we frustrate ourselves with inconsequential matters, we would find much wasted time. On the other hand, leaving matters in God's hands is time management in itself. God deals with all matters at the right time. The principle by which we abide is taking things to God in prayer instead of using our own understanding and ability to solve these problems.

The word *time* has several meanings, including the following:

- "A point or period of times"
- "The right or agreed moment to do something"
- "An indefinite period"
- "An instance of something happening or being done"

Time management is crucial to man. We may not be perfect, but we live a life where time is essential. Keep your timing to a minimum and leave the rest to God to handle. He is sovereign and knows best. He will make things right at the appointed time. Lean on God for understanding in His timing!

An anointing is on everyone who believes God is approachable and that we can ask the Father for anything and He will answer our prayer according to His will. We do not have to act as predominant people, thinking we can solve every problem. We have to live by the principles guiding our lives.

Anointing is the principle of teaching someone that God is able to handle things that we humans are unable to handle—the essence of life. The anointing is on everyone, but the manifestation of it is different in everybody. Time requires the anointing to be able to withhold oneself from making the wrong choices. Greater is the man who leans on the wisdom and integrity of God; his life would be like a huge pile of anointing. He will speak with wisdom at all times.

With time, God will heal all wounds. *"Happy are those who mourn; God will comfort them!* (Matthew 5:4). With time, God will make things right for the mourner. With time, things will change for the better.

The Principle of Unity

The noun *unity* has the following meanings:

- The state of being united or forming a whole
- Come or bring together for a common purpose or to form a whole
- A thing forming a complex whole

"Happy are those who work for peace; God will call them his children! – Matthew 5:9

Togetherness, which is oneness in God, is bringing all people together in God. The principle of unity is the principle that brings us together to fulfill the will of God. The principle of time is associated with the principle of unity. With time, all things become possible, and with time, we will enjoy what God intended for us.

Time is the leader of all. With time, all things will be achieved in God's kingdom. For the unification of mankind, we must have peace on earth. We work for peace in bringing us together in the Lord. God is peace-loving! He's all about bringing people together! Unity is the principle for God's people working for peace in the Lord.

Unity is the word!

The Principle of Adoration

Adoration has the following meanings:

- A feeling of profound love and admiration
- The act of admiring adoration strongly—the act of admiring strongly

- The worship given to God alone

We worship God with our whole heart and fall deeply in love with Him. *"Happy are the pure in heart; they will see God!* (Matthew 5:8).

The pure in heart adore God and worship Him fervently. They fear God in everything they do and put Him first in their lives. Also, they consider God before anyone else, and are God-seeking people with a heart for the Creator.

The Principle of Equalities

The word *equalities* mean the following:

- The quality of being the same in quantity or measure or value or status
- *Sameness* means "the quality of being alike." i.e., "sameness of purpose kept them together"
- A state of being essentially equal or equivalent; equally balanced
- A person or thing that is equal to another; no difference

This principle is one of being non-judgmental. Everyone is judged the same. These are the merciful in the Lord! *"Happy are those who are merciful to others; God will be merciful to them!* (Matthew 5:7).

The Principle of Nationalism

The word *nationalism* has several meanings, which include the following:

- The love of country and willingness to sacrifice for it
- The doctrine that your national culture and interests are superior to any other
- The spirit or aspirations of a country
- A devotion to the interests of one's own country
- A desire for national advancement
- The policy of asserting the interest of one's own nation, as separate from the interest of another nation and the common interest of all nations

In this context, some are persecuted for the love of their country and what they believe in. They will protect and defend their religion for the sake of love and unity. All nations shall strive against me, but I will stand fast in the name of Jesus for His glory to come true.

Condemnation from others will not stop me. I love my church and will stand by it to the end.

"Happy are those who are persecuted because they do what God requires; the Kingdom of heaven belongs to them! (Matthew 5:10).

All the nations that you have created will come and bow down to you; they will praise your greatness (Psalm 86:9).

The Principle of Remuneration

Remuneration has several meanings, which include the following:

- Something given in exchange for goods or services rendered.
- Payment for work done.
- Something to make up for loss or damage.

This principle talks about gratification. *"Happy are those whose greatest desire is to do what God requires; God will satisfy them fully!* (Matthew 5:6).

The Principle of Faith

The word *faith* means all of the following:

- A strong or unshakeable belief in something, especially without proof or evidence
- A specific system of religious beliefs: the Jewish faith
- (Theology) Christianity; trust in God and in His actions and promises
- (Theology) a conviction of the truth of certain doctrines of religion, esp. when this is not based on reason
- Complete confidence or trust in a person, remedy, etc.
- Any set of firmly held principles or beliefs
- Allegiance or loyalty, as to a person or cause

"Happy are those who know they are spiritually poor; the Kingdom of heaven belongs to them! (Matthew 5:3).

A conviction of the truth speaks about faith—the word that everyone seemingly dreads. Talking about faith is a whole concept of truth. You teach faith, and the entire congregation changes their faith in you. Faith is quite a topic with which to be reckoned. It is massive, but the Word of God is great in identifying loopholes and covering them with love. Faith rescues people, and faith brings people to God. The elimination of baggage from the past brings faith in God. Faith is such an expansive concept to address that the fourth chapter of this book will be dedicated solely to the subject. The chapter will address your faith in God, lessons to be learned and why God loves us the way He does.

Faith is why when Jesus died on the cross, the curtain in the temple that separates the Holy Place from the Most Holy Place (Exodus 26:31-33) was torn in two, starting from the top of the curtain (Matthew 27:51). This shows that the Church has to learn the principles of the Lord from the beginning to the end, and the beginning starts from the base of the cross. The legitimate sign of the cross is to bring peace to the children of God; therefore, the reason Jesus had to die on that cross was to bring us peace within us. He has to build the Church from the beginning to the end. The Church is all about Jesus and His laws.

In Conclusion

The Church is built upon Jesus [the Rock] and His principles—the ones that came with Him to the cross. He lived with us on earth, and through us, came to the cross for salvation. He delivered us from our stress and brought salvation to our door. The world will live to see the salvation of the Lord manifest in us, but the generation that will live their lives according to the will of the world will see their world disintegrated into the Enemy's world. The sign of the Devil is coming; you have seen it, and it is coming. The world is in shock at what is happening, but it is due to happen as the generation is not concerned about God's Word. They live their lives as if there is no God and worship gods of other natures.

The lampstand is a representative of the Son of God—Jesus Christ in the churches, who is to bring oneness in the Church. It stands for who you are in the Church and bases its theory on the management of the churches within the Church. The churches are in breach of God's Word, and the only way to bring them together is to follow the Word of God in their life, which is Jesus Christ the Resurrection. He will resurrect the Church through His word of wisdom and His intelligence. He will invade the churches and make them as merciful as can be. He will teach His Word to the congregation and bring peace to this world, but the word is,

- *Who is about to listen to Him because He comes in His outermost self to preach the Word?*

- *Which of you is prepared to listen to Him as the world is in chaos?*
- *Will you learn His Word to you?"*

The Church has been splintered and needs to come together as one, but how will that happen with the whole world marching against God and His message? Live according to the Word of God and bring peace to the world of chaos. The world will face its critical moment of recession as all of its assets will be lost to the Enemy, bringing depression into the world. In fact, all the assets of the world will vanish into the hands of the Enemy, but the Word of the Lord will remain standing. The Word says you should leave all of your burdens on Him, Jesus Christ, and He will carry them to the cross for you. You cannot fight the Enemy of old, but you can leave him in the hands of the Lord Jesus Christ, who will banish him from the land of the living. He has created a grave for him where he will live for eternity.

This world is about to experience a great famine that will bring man to his knees to seek the face of God. In doing so, the Lord will bring His Son, Jesus Christ (*the son to be given to us*) to us to save us in the end. He shall bring restoration to the world and save us from the hands of the Enemy. Restoration is in the Word of God; it shows us who we are in the Lord and what makes us who we are.

The lampstand stands in the Tent of the LORD's presence where the curtain divides us from the throne room [the Holy of Holies], but this curtain is temporary and needs to be shredded. The Lord is the ultimate God who can shred this blindness from our eyes. So, God sent His Son, Jesus Christ, the Restorer of our soul, to bring us closer to the LORD.

- He brought us closer to the Lord, but who is prepared to leave his life in place of the life of Christ?

No one because we instead choose to live our lives in chaos—a way that is unpleasant to the Lord, pretending to be someone we are not. Bringing this life to the table of God would be a disaster. So, the Lord brought His own Son, Jesus Christ, to save us from that disaster we call life.

The resurrection of the saints is to bring discipline in the Church. You cannot bring discipline in the Church without resurrecting the saints—the reason Jesus had to die first before the curtain split in two from the top. It would not have happened if Jesus had died before His time.

That is why it is necessary to teach the Word of God before resurrecting the crowd. You cannot give them the Word of God after resurrection; it has to go hand in hand: deliver and resurrect.

- On what will believers stand when you resurrect them without the Word of God?

They need the basis of the Word to stand on—the rock to stabilize them (Matthew 16:18-20).

And so I tell you, Peter: you are a rock, and on this rock foundation I will build my church, and not even death will ever be able to overcome it (Matthew 16:18).

The lampstand stands in the Holy Place of the tabernacle with all the other items of worship (the table of showbread and the golden altar of incense). By looking at the table, you will find who the Lord is among His Church.

- Who is the Lord among His Church?

He is the Word of God among His people. He teaches God's Word to the people and gets them converted. He teaches His Word according to the will of God; hearing the Word of God brings conviction to people. He is the Ancient of days, the Maker of heaven and earth, the Restorer of our faith, the I Am that I Am, the Faith of God, the Generations of God, and the Deliverer of our soul.

The lampstand represents Christ in us, the Commander of our will. He replaces Himself with us and teaches His Word through us—that is the Savior we serve and would be if we let Him reign in us.

The next book in the series is titled *Perfect Adoration,* and it addresses the depression in our walk with God, the solution to our depression, and the reason for us to follow Jesus Christ.

Thanks for reading!

www.euniceforson.org

#theoneness

SHE SHIFTED!
"She changed her position as the woman with the issue of blood to the daughter of Jesus."
AVAILABLE AT
amazon
Available in Kindle and Paperback

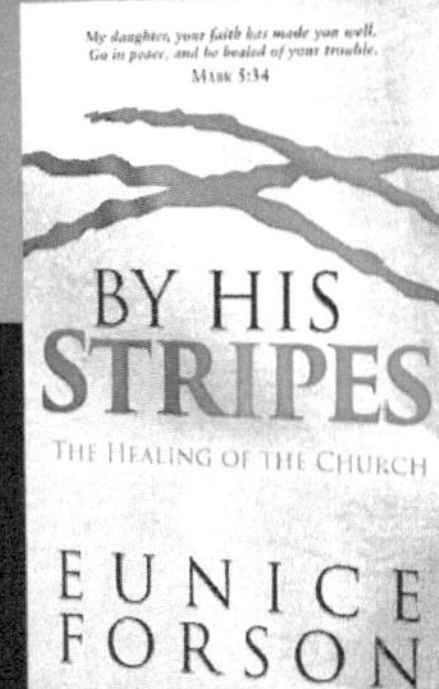

My daughter, your faith has made you well. Go in peace, and be healed of your trouble.
MARK 5:34
BY HIS STRIPES
THE HEALING OF THE CHURCH
EUNICE FORSON

Other Books by Eunice Forson

By His Stripes

Perfect Adoration: Overcoming depression in the church

A review for *The Oneness* would be greatly appreciated.
Kindly leave one!